AUGUSTINE OF HIPPO

HARPERCOLLINS SPIRITUAL CLASSICS:

John of the Cross
Teresa of Avila
The Cloud of Unknowing
John and Charles Wesley
Meister Eckhart
Bonaventure: The Life of St. Francis
William Law
Quaker Spirituality
Bernard of Clairvaux
Hildegard of Bingen
Augustine of Hippo
Francis & Clare of Assisi

AUGUSTINE OF HIPPO

Selected Writings

Foreword by Francine du Plessix Gray

Edited by Emilie Griffin

Translation by Mary T. Clark

HarperSanFrancisco

A Division of HarperCollins*Publishers*

HarperCollins books may be purchased for educational, business, or sales promotional use. For information please write: Special Markets Department, HarperCollins Publishers, 10 East 53rd Street, New York, NY 10022.

HarperCollins Web site: http://www.harpercollins.com
HarperCollins®, ♦®, and HarperSanFrancisco™ are trademarks of HarperCollins Publishers

Book Design by Susan Rimerman

FIRST EDITION

Library of Congress Cataloging-in-Publication Data.
Augustine, Saint, Bishop of Hippo.
  [Selections. English. 2006]
  Augustine of Hippo: selected writings / foreword by Francine du Plessix Gray. — 1st ed.
    p. cm. — (HarperCollins spiritual classics)
ISBN–13: 978–0–06–075466–2
ISBN–10: 0–06–075466–4
    1. Theology. 2. Sermons, Latin—Translations into English. I. Title. II. Series.
BR65.A52E6 2006
270.2–dc22

                                                            2005056405

06 07 08 09 10 RRD(H) 10 9 8 7 6 5 4 3 2 1

CONTENTS

FOREWORD

Imagine a waning empire—third-century Rome—so afflicted with spiritual anxiety that its emperor, Alexander Severus, keeps statues of Abraham, Orpheus, and Christ in his private chapel. Upon the decline of paganism, a frantic search for self-help pervades the Mediterranean world and breeds a proliferation of religious cults: Gnostics, Manicheans, Donatists all vie for converts, but by the mid-fourth century a particularly popular sect called Christianity is gaining disciples at a brisker pace than any other persuasion. Demanding a far more ardent commitment than other affiliations, it wields a bigger stick than its rivals but offers a juicier, more democratic carrot. It requires no social or educational distinction or previous level of education. And unlike the pale, fasting, self-absorbed Manichean elders, Christian leaders generously provide for their followers—care for widows, orphans, the disabled, or the unemployed. Its inclusiveness, charity, and promises of heavenly reward are such that it seems to be the only religion worth dying for, and even the pagan emperor Marcus Aurelius writes with emotion of the courage displayed by Christian martyrs when confronted with death.

It is in the North African part of this anxious late empire, some forty-two miles south of Carthage, in a small town called Thagaste (present-day Souk Akras, Algeria), that Saint Augustine of Hippo, the greatest thinker of Christian antiquity, was born. The year was 354, four decades after Emperor Constantine had offered Christianity a privileged status throughout the empire. Augustine's parents were a modest petit bourgeois couple; his father, a tax collector, was pagan, his mother, Monica, was a devout Christian. Baptism, in those centuries, was exclusively reserved for adults, so there was no question of little Augustine being baptized in his mother's faith.

By the time he was sixteen, Augustine showed signs of being an intellectual prodigy, and his parents found a wealthy patron willing to underwrite his higher education. The most prestigious vocation a bright young man could then aspire to was that of orator: the uniquely privileged status of *Vir eloquentissimus* had prevailed throughout the classical world for several centuries, and Augustine was sent to Carthage, the Paris of North Africa, to train for this most distinguished of callings.

And what a skilled orator Augustine became! At the age of nineteen he was already teaching the art of rhetoric in Carthage, "[selling] the power of speaking," (p. 15). as he put it; he felt assured enough in his social standing to take a concubine, to whom he would be faithful for thirteen years and who would bear him a very cherished son (in his *Confessions*, Augustine tends to exaggerate his sinfulness: such unions were then seen as totally respectable for any *homme moyen sensuel*). In those same years he joined the Manicheans, a popular dualistic sect that believed the universe was governed by two conflicting forces—the powers of Evil incarnated in Matter and the powers of Good incarnated in Spirit. Augustine's success as teacher and orator was such that at the age of twenty-nine, after traveling to Italy with his mother, common-law wife, and son, he was offered the most prestigious chair of rhetoric in Milan, then the capital of the Roman Empire: such a position would be roughly equivalent to becoming today, at the same age, the chair of Goldman Sachs or the president of Harvard University.

It is ironic that Augustine, in his *Confessions*, traces the start of his tortuous journey toward God to his reading of two pagan authors, Cicero and, later, Plotinus. Convinced by these sages to dedicate his life to the search for "an immortality of wisdom," * while still teaching in Milan, he foreswore his allegiance to the Manichean sect and took a vow of asceticism, shipping his concubine back to Africa. His first interest in Christianity can be traced to his impassioned admiration for the sermons of the great Saint Ambrose, bishop of Milan. The pivotal moment of his conversion occurred in 386, in the extraordinary "Tolle Legge" episode described in Chapter VIII of his *Confessions*; it is then that the voice of an unseen child, singing the phrase "Take and read, take and read." incited him to peruse a passage of the apostle Paul, which urged him to "Put on the Lord Jesus Christ." Soon afterward he was baptized by Saint Ambrose in a baptistry one can see to this day in the underground tunnels of the Milan cathedral, and he resigned his prestigious chair of rhetoric. Thus tuned in and dropped out, to use our 1960s lingo, Augustine settled down, at the age of thirty-three, to the modest existence of a celibate, contemplative intellectual.

Upon the death of his beloved mother—the deep grief he felt upon this loss strengthened his resolve to lead a monastic life—

---

* From the complete *The Confessions of Saint Augustine*, Modern English Version, by Hal M. Helms, Paraclete Press, Orleans, Mass., 1986. Other quotations without other citation are taken from this translation.

Augustine returned to his native Africa, hoping to found a religious community. But by this time Emperor Theodosius had
made Christianity the official religion of the empire, and the
shortage of pastors was acute. Augustine was ordained, under
popular pressure, to serve as priest in Hippo, a large seaside city
second only to Carthage in importance. And four years later, aged
forty-one, he was made the city's bishop. (One should see this
promotion in the relatively humble context of the times: there
were already seven hundred bishops in Africa alone, and they
wore the stark, rough-hewn vestments now associated with contemporary monks.) For the next few decades Augustine com-
bined the administrative duties of his bishopric with an
astoundingly prolific preaching and writing schedule. He died in
AD 430, at the age of seventy-six, just as a horde of invading Van-
dals, closing in on his city of Hippo, were putting an end to the
culture of Christian antiquity in which Augustine's genius had
blazed.

Only in Augustine, the major bridge between pagan and Christian thought, do we get a full first-person account of the tensions
and clashes that these two contrasting views of humankind
wrought in one man. Only through his writings can we intimately
witness the fusion of New Testament religion with the Platonic tradition of Greek philosophy, a fusion that would become the basis
of medieval Roman Catholicism and of Renaissance Protestantism.
If one were to cite just a few of Augustine's doctrinal contributions
to Christian thought, they would include the following: Abolishing the mind/body dualism so prevalent in the first centuries of

our era, he presented a worldview that held spirit has primacy over matter, but emphasized that matter, as God's creation, has its own sacredness. Making amends for those years he had spent "intoxicated with Manichean vanities," he followed Plotinus in denying that evil had any substantive existence and asserting that it should merely be seen as the privation of good. He resolved the thorny issue of the world's creation by positing that only God can create ex nihilo and bring forth time out of eternity. And he established the foundations for the doctrine of the Trinity and the doctrine of Grace as they are still known in most mainstream Christian denominations.

But there are many secular concepts that one can equally attribute to Augustine. Uncommonly aware of the motivations of the self, he created the first modern concept of the human will, and his extraordinary capacity to analyze intimate and complex emotions brings him closer than most any pre-Renaissance thinker to our modern sensibility. The first philosopher to speculate on the basic principles of human psychology, he was a pioneering theoretician of memory, describing it, in one of his typically colorful metaphors, as "the belly of the mind," and he may well have been the first to inaugurate the concept of what we now know as the human subconscious. Moreover, in the question he so often poses—"Who am I then, O my God?"—he might also be seen as our first existentialist. It is not insignificant that in 1932, a young Jewish scholar at the University of Berlin called Hannah Arendt chose to write her doctoral dissertation on Saint Augustine's doctrine of love.

Over the past twenty-five years, I've read and reread Saint Augustine's *Confessions* in Roman libraries, on Caribbean beaches, in hospital beds, in student-filled classrooms, on airplanes bound for Tokyo, in Parisian cafés. The warm intimacy of his voice and the candor of his self-revelations ("an unaffected candor," as a college professor of mine once put it, "which would seldom be found in a bartender") compel me to look on him as the Absolute Friend who never fails to give me joy and solace. Each new reading heightens my sense of humanity's wretchedness and potential glory and offers new insights into our propensity for destruction and the complex motivations of our psyches. Moreover, what writer would not delight in the sumptuous incantational rhythm, which Augustine derived from his intensive study of the Psalms? Who of us would not find pleasure in the rich, witty metaphoric language characteristic of an African tradition that excelled at picaresque details, at puns and riddles, at pithy paradoxes "So small a boy and so great a sinner"; "I came to Carthage, where a caldron of unholy loves bubbled up all around me"; "Give me chastity and continence, but not yet"?

Let me share one more insight bequeathed me by Saint Augustine, which has been particularly precious to my craft as a writer: Having enjoyed a brilliant career hawking, as he puts it, "the art of speaking for sale," upon tuning in and dropping out, Augustine realized that his society's adulation of rhetoric had turned his colleagues into a society of corrupt hot air artists. It is only when he abandoned his lucrative word-peddling job and followed the apostle Paul's directive to put on the Word of

Christ—capital *W*—that he was able to find those "words of the soul" with which he wrote his timeless works. I read my own literary implications into this conversion: Augustine has led me to believe that there is a particular form of grace to be sought by those of us who aspire to true literature; that it is our duty, as authors, to disdain the language of the marketplace and follow an ethic of the sign—or to put a gloss on one of the Ten Commandments, "Honor Thy Medium as Thyself." He has taught me that all those verbal devices that his colleagues in the art of rhetoric pioneered—simile, metaphor, irony, apostrophe—must be used with frugal, tender precision, advice that could well be heeded by the contemporary writer seeking to make fast lucre by resorting to the hype of mass media or by disdaining the distinction between fiction and nonfiction. If I get him right, Augustine of Hippo intimates, however obliquely, that writers worth their salt have it in them to acquire the grace of the word: "Too late have I loved You, O beauty, ancient yet ever new . . . and behold You were within, but I was outside" (p.52).

—FRANCINE DU PLESSIX GRAY

CONFESSIONS

Shortly after Augustine became bishop, he was asked by Paulinus of Nola to write his confessions. About this work Augustine wrote: "The thirteen books of my Confessions, dealing with my evil and good deeds, give praise to the just and good God, and also awaken man's mind and heart to Him."

The first nine books describe how Divine Providence worked in the first thirty-three years of Augustine's life to open him to God. The tenth book reveals the spiritual state of Augustine after his conversion and at the time he was writing this book. It is a gloriously frank self-examination wherein the struggle and conflict of Christian life are squarely faced with the confidence given by grace and hope. The last three books represent meditations on Scripture leading to personal reflections on time and eternity, creation and reconciliation, transfiguration and the restoration of all things in the Word of God, through whom they were created.

In the first book of the Confessions Augustine's great religious discovery was: "You have made us to be 'toward' you, and our heart is restless until it rests in you." Augustine strongly desires the peace that comes from rest in God and leads to prayer, God's gift to those who acknowledge their need, their spiritual restlessness, for Him. This happiness of repose arrives fully only in the heavenly Jerusalem to those who have opened their wounds to the healing power of Christ, the "humble Physician."

Included here, Book 8 vividly describes the moral influence of fervent Christians on Augustine, the tale of the unexpected conversion of Victorinus, and Augustine's sudden moral conversion. In Book 9 a son describes the influence of a Christian mother and recalls the ecstasy at Ostia of mother and son. In Book 10 Augustine explains his motivation for writing the Confessions and analyzes human memory, which will be an appropriate foundation for his Image doctrine in a later excerpt from On the Trinity. After a prayer of confidence to

God, he confesses the temptations to which he is still subject from the lust of the flesh, the lust of the eyes, and the pride of life. But he also admits to moments of experiencing God that "if made permanent would be hard to distinguish from the life to come."

His hope, however, is firmly placed not in these transitory religious experiences but rather in Christ the Mediator.

—MARY T. CLARK

Book 8

My God, let me remember you with gratitude, and confess your mercies to me. Let my bones be penetrated with your love and exclaim: "Lord, who is like unto you? You have broken my bonds: I shall offer you a sacrifice of praise" (Ps 86:8). And how you have broken them I shall narrate, and upon hearing this all those who adore you will say: Blessed be the Lord both in heaven and on earth; great and wonderful is His name. Your words had become deeply rooted in my heart and I was "surrounded on all sides by you" (Jb 1:10). I was now certain of your eternal life, although I saw it "through a glass darkly" (1 Cor 13:12), as it were; yet all my doubt concerning incorruptible substance, from which all other substance came, was removed, nor did I desire to be more certain of you but to stand more firmly in you.

As for my own temporal life all things were tottering, and "my heart had to be purged from old leaven" (1 Cor 5:7). The way, the Savior Himself, delighted me, but I was still unwilling to enter His narrow way. But you inspired me, and it seemed good to me to go to Simplicianus, who seemed to me to be your good servant, and in him your grace shone forth. I had also heard that from his youth he had lived devoutly for you; now he was grown old; and it seemed to me that from a long life of steadfastly following your way he must have experienced much and learned much. And he truly had. Hence after disclosing to him my troubles, I wished him to suggest from his experience and learning the most appropriate way for someone with my sentiments to begin to follow you.

For I saw the Church full; and one went this way, and another that way. But it was displeasing to me that I acted like a worldling, and it was greatly burdensome to me now that the hope of honor and of money no longer inflamed my desires as it formerly did to help me endure such a heavy bondage. For those hopes no longer delighted me when compared with the sweetness and beauty of your house, which I loved. But I was still strongly bound to a woman; nor did the Apostle forbid me to marry (1 Cor 7:8), although he exhorted to a better state, greatly desirous as he was that all men should be as he himself was. But I, weaker than he, chose the softer place; and on that account my life was in confusion because I languished and pined away with growing anxieties, because there were many things I was unwilling to suffer but had to put up with for the sake of living with a wife, a way of life to which I was bound. I had heard from the mouth of Truth itself that "there were some eunuchs who had made themselves such on account of the Kingdom of Heaven; but, he said, let whoever can take this, take it" (Mt 19:12). Certainly "all those men are vain in whom there is no knowledge of God, and who could not from those things which are good discover Him who is" (2 Ws 13:1). But I was no longer in that vanity: I had transcended it, and by the common witness of all your creation I had discovered you, our Creator, and your Word, God with you, and with you one God, through whom you had created all things. There is also another kind of impiety, that of those who "knowing God, did not glorify Him as God or give thanks" (Rom 1:21). Among these also I had fallen, but your right hand sustained me both deserved and received a statue in the Roman Forum (which citizens of this world consider an honor)—up to old age he had worshiped idols and joined in those sacrilegious rites which were the fashion with almost all the Roman nobility, who had inflamed the people with their enthusiasm for Osiris and the dog Anubis and that monstrous brood of deity which once took arms and fought in arms against Minerva, Neptune, Venus— gods which Rome had once conquered and whom she now adored. And for all these years old Victorinus with his thundering eloquence had been the defender of these gods; yet he did not blush to become the child of your Christ, an infant at your font, submitting his neck to the yoke of humility and submitting his forehead to the scandal of the Cross.

O Lord, Lord, you "who have lowered the heavens and descended, touched the mountains and they smoked" (Ps 144:5), by what means did you make your way into the heart of that man? He read, as Simplicianus said, the holy Scriptures, and he most studiously investigated and searched through all the Christian writings and said to Simplicianus not publicly but privately as friend to friend: "I should like you to know that I am now a Christian." And Simplicianus answered: "I shall not believe nor shall I count you as a Christian unless I see you in the Church of Christ." But, smiling, Victorinus said: "Do walls therefore make Christians?" And he often repeated that he was a Christian, and Simplicianus just as often answered in the same way, and Victorinus would make the same retort about "the walls." For he feared to offend his friends who were important

people and devil worshipers: From the height of their Babylon-
ian dignity, as from the height of the cedars of Lebanon, which
the Lord had not yet brought down, he thought a storm of ill
will would fall upon him. But when by reading and desire he
had gained strength, he grew afraid that Christ might deny him
before His angels if he feared to confess Christ before men. He
saw himself guilty of a great crime by being ashamed of the
Sacraments of the humility of your Word while not having been
ashamed of the sacrilegious rites of those proud devils whom as
a proud follower he had worshiped. So he turned his pride
against what was vain and became humble toward the truth.
Suddenly, without warning, he said to the surprised Simplicianus: "Let us go to the church: I want to be made a Christian."
And Simplicianus, overcome with joy, went along with him.
When he was instructed in the first Sacraments, he gave his
name as one who wished to be reborn through baptism. Rome
marveled and the church rejoiced. The proud "saw and were
indignant, they gnashed their teeth and pined away with grief";
but you, Lord God, were the hope of your servant and he "did
not look back at vanities and lying follies" (Ps 39:5).

Finally, when the hour had arrived for his profession of faith in
a set formula from a platform in the sight of the faithful people, as
was the custom at Rome for those about to come to your grace,
Simplicianus told me that the priests had offered Victorinus the
opportunity of making his profession in private, as the custom
was with those who seemed likely to be frightened or embar-
rassed by the public ceremony. But he chose rather to profess his

salvation in the sight of the church congregation. For there had been no salvation in the rhetoric that he taught, and yet he had professed it publicly. How much less, therefore, should he fear your meek flock in proclaiming your Word, he who did not fear proclaiming his own words before the crowds of madmen? And so when he ascended the platform to make his profession, all who knew him (and was there anyone who did not?) whispered his name to one another with glad murmurs. From the lips of the rejoicing congregation sounded the whisper: "Victorinus, Victorinus." Quickly they spoke with exultation when they saw him, and quickly they became silent so that they might hear him. He proclaimed aloud the true faith with glorious confidence, and they all wished to draw him within their very hearts. Indeed, they did take him to their hearts by their love and rejoicing: These were the hands by which they clasped him.

3

O loving God, what in man makes him rejoice more over the salvation of a soul that has been despaired of, of one delivered from a major danger, than if there had always been hope for him or if the danger had been less great? Indeed, even you, merciful Father, "rejoice more over a penitent than over ninety-nine just persons who have no need of repentance" (Lk 15:7). And it is with great joy also that we heard how the lost sheep was brought home again upon the shoulders of the exultant shepherd, and how the lost coin was replaced in your treasury, her neighbors rejoicing with the woman who found it. And the joy experienced

at your church Liturgy brings tears as we hear read the parable of
the younger son who was dead and brought back to life, who
had been lost and was found (Lk 15:11–32). Indeed, you rejoice
over us as also over your angels, who are steadfast in holy charity. For you are always the same because you know in the same
manner all those realities which themselves neither are always
existent nor always the same.

What is it in the soul, I again ask, that makes it more delighted
to have found or regained those things which it loved than if it
had always possessed them? There are many other examples of
this; indeed, the evidence everywhere proclaims that this is so.
The general triumphs as a conqueror, but he would not have conquered unless he had fought, and the greater danger there was in
battle, so much the more rejoicing is there in the triumph. The
storm tosses the sailors and threatens shipwreck; everyone grows
pale at the approach of death: But the sky and sea grow tranquil,
and as they have exceedingly feared, they exceedingly rejoice. A
dear friend is sick, and his pulse reveals that he is in danger. All
who want him healthy are likewise sympathetically sick with
him; he recovers, although not yet walking with his former
strength, and there is more joy than there was previously when
he was well and perfectly able to walk. We procure the very pleasures of our human life by way of pain, not only unexpected pain
and contrary to our wills but even unpleasantness planned and
willingly accepted. There is no pleasure in eating and drinking
unless the vexation of hunger and thirst precedes it. Drunkards
eat certain salty things to bring about an uncomfortable dryness,

But if they are less well known among the people, those who know them also rejoice less. For when many rejoice together, the joy of each one is fuller because they warm themselves at one another's flame. Finally, because they are known by many, they guide many to salvation and are sure to be followed by many. Even those preceding them on the same way feel great joy, and not only for them. Far be it that in your tabernacle the persons of the rich should be more welcome than the poor, or the noble before the common people, since you have chosen the weak things of this world to confound the mighty, and "you have chosen the base and contemptible things and those things which are not but should be to bring to naught the things which are" (1 Cor 1:27). You spoke those words by the tongue of the "least" of your Apostles. Yet, when Paulus the Proconsul had his pride overcome by the spiritual warfare of the Apostle and was put under the easy yoke of Christ, now made a humble subject of the Great King, he also desired to be called Paul instead of Saul, which was his previous name—as a sign of so great a victory. For the enemy is more overcome in that victory of a man over whom he had greater hold and by whom he held many others. But he had more hold on the proud by reason of their nobility and of many more through them by reason of their authority.

Therefore the heart of Victorinus was all the more welcome because the devil had held it as an invincible fortress, and the tongue of Victorinus because it was a strong, keen weapon by which the devil had slain many. It was right for your sons to rejoice very specially because our King had bound the strong spirit against the flesh" (Gal 5:17). I no doubt was on both sides, but I was more myself on that side which I approved of for myself than when I was on that of which I disapproved for myself. For I myself was no longer on the latter side, because for the most part I suffered against my will rather than did it willingly. Yet habit had grown stronger against me by my own help because I had come willingly where I was unwilling now to be. And who then can rightly complain when just punishment overtakes the sinner? And I no longer had that excuse by which it seemed to me that I could not forsake the world to follow you because the knowledge of truth was for me uncertain. By now I was quite certain. But I was still tied down to earth and refused to accept service in your army. I was as much afraid of being freed from what hindered my going to you as I should have feared whatever might hinder this. So I was as pleasantly weighed down by the baggage of this world as one often is in sleep. And the thoughts by which I meditated on you were like the struggles of someone desirous to get up and yet overcome by a deep sleep, falling back again into it. There is no one who wishes to sleep always since according to everyone's sound judgment it is better to be awake; nevertheless a man postpones shaking off his drowsiness when there is a heavy sluggishness in his body, and although it displeases him he willingly settles in to another doze although he knows the time for rising has come. In like manner I was certain that it was better for me to commit myself to your love rather than to yield to my sensuality; but although the former course was pleasing and convincing, the latter delighted my act of friendship had agreed to lecture under Verecundus, a great friend of ours, a citizen and elementary-school master of Milan who eagerly wanted Nebridius's assistance and by the right of friendship even demanded from one of our group the faithful aid which he greatly needed. Nebridius was not drawn to this by any desire of profit—for he could have done better for himself by teaching literature, if he pleased—but as a good and gentle friend he was too kindly a man to turn down our request. But he did it very discreetly, desirous of being unknown to persons of worldly reputation, avoiding all disturbance of mind, for he wished to have a free mind and as many hours of leisure as possible to seek or read or hear truths concerning wisdom.

Therefore on a certain day—I do not recall why Nebridius was absent—behold there came to our house, to me and Alypius, a certain Ponticianus, our fellow-citizen, an African, holder of an important office at the court of the emperor. He had something or other he wanted from us, and we sat down to talk about it. Nearby was a game table, and he happened to notice the book lying there; he took it, opened it, and found it to be the Apostle Paul, certainly contrary to what he expected to find; for he thought it would be one of those books I wore myself out teaching. Smiling then and gazing closely at me, he expressed pleasure as well as surprise that I had this book and only this book at my side. For he was a Christian and a faithful one, and often prostrated himself before you, our God, in church in daily prayers, and many times daily. I indicated to him that I was greatly concerned with those Scriptures. Then he began to tell the story of

Anthony the monk of Egypt, whose name was esteemed among
your servants although we had not until then heard of him. When
he discovered this, he talked about him all the more, eager to
make known so great a man to those who knew him not, and
very much marveling at our ignorance. But Alypius and I were
amazed to hear of your wonderful works, done in the true faith
and in the Catholic Church so recently, indeed, practically in our
own time and witnessed to by so many. We all marveled—we,
that such great things were done, he, that we had never heard of
them before.

He went on to speak of the great groups living in monasteries,
of their way of life, which was full of the sweet fragrance of you,
and of the fruitful deserts in the wilderness, of which we knew
nothing. There was actually a monastery at Milan, outside the city
walls. It was full of good brethren and was under Ambrose's direction, and we had never heard of it. He continued to speak and we
listened intently. Then he began to say that he and three other com-
rades—I know not when—at Treves when the emperor was busy
with circus chariot races, went walking in the gardens near the
city walls; and it so happened that they separated into two groups,
one walking with him and the other two going off by themselves.
But as these two were wandering up and down, they stumbled by
chance upon a certain small house where dwelt some of your servants, "poor in spirit, of which is the Kingdom of Heaven" (Mt
5:5), and they found there a book in which was written the Life of
Anthony. One of the two began to read it, to marvel and be
inflamed, and while reading to ponder on his own living of such

a life and forsaking his military pursuits, serving you. For these two men were both officials in the emperor's civil service. Then suddenly filled with holy love, and a sober shame, angry with himself, he looked at his friend and said: "Tell me, I beg you, for what post of honor are we striving with all our labors? What are we seeking? Why are we serving the State? Can our hopes in court rise higher than to become the emperor's friends? And is not such a place insecure and full of danger? And through how many dangers must we go to arrive at a greater danger? And how long will it take to get there? But if I want, I can be the friend of God now, this moment." He said this, and, perplexed in the labor of a new life to which he was giving birth, he looked again at the book. He read on and was inwardly changed where you alone could see; and his mind was emptied of worldly affairs, as was soon made evident. For while he read and the waves of his heart rose and fell, he expressed his self-anger, saw the better way, and chose it for himself. And having become yours, he said to his friend: "Now I have torn myself from those hopes of ours, and have decided to serve God; and this—from this moment in this place I shall undertake. If you are unwilling to imitate me, do not dissuade me." The other answered that he would remain his companion in so great a service for so great a prize. And both, now yours, built a spiritual tower at the only adequate cost, that of leaving all things and following you.

Then Ponticianus and the one with him who had walked through other parts of the garden seeking for their friends came upon them and warned that they should return because the day

was ending. But they declared to them their resolutions and purpose and told them how that will had arisen in them and was
now fixed, and they begged their friends, if they would not join
them, not to interfere with their purpose. Ponticianus and his
friend, though not changed from their former state, nevertheless
wept, for themselves, as he told us, piously wishing them well
and recommending themselves to their prayers; and with their
hearts still turned toward earthly things, they returned to the
court. But the other two, with their hearts fixed on heaven,
remained in that cottage. And both of them were to be married;
when their fiancées heard what had happened, they also dedicated their virginity to you.

7

This was the story Ponticianus told. But you, O Lord, while he was
speaking turned me around to face myself, taking me from
behind my back, where I had placed myself when I was reluctant
to see myself; and you set me in front of my own face that I might
see how deformed, how crooked and sordid, stained and ulcerous
I was. I saw and I was horrified and found no way to flee from
myself. And if I tried to turn away my gaze from myself, he continued to relate this story. And you set me in front of myself and
thrust me before my own eyes so that I might discover my iniquity and hate it. I was aware of it, but I pretended to be unaware. I
deliberately looked the other way and dropped it from my mind.

Then indeed the more ardently I loved those young men as I
heard of their determination to win health for their souls by giving

themselves totally to your healing, the more bitterly I hated myself
in comparison with them: since I had already squandered so many
years—about twelve—since my nineteenth year, when, having read
Cicero's *Hortensius*, I was first stirred up to study wisdom, and I was
still postponing the contempt of earthly happiness and the inquiry
into that of which not only the finding but even the search should
have been preferred before the already found treasures and king-
doms of this world and before all bodily pleasures readily available.
But I, wretched young man that I was, even more wretched in my
early youth, had begged chastity from you and had said: "Give me
chastity and continence but not yet." For I feared that you would
hear me too soon and too soon deliver me from my disease of concupiscence, which I wrongly desired to have satisfied rather than
extinguished. And I had gone along evil ways, following a sacrilegious superstition through the wicked ways of Manichaeism not
because I was convinced by it but because I preferred it to the Christian teachings into which I did not inquire in a religious spirit but
merely opposed in a spirit of malice.

I had thought that the reason I postponed from day to day forsaking worldly hope to follow you was only because there did
not seem any certain goal to which to direct my course. But now
the day had come when I stood naked in my own sight and when
my own conscience accused me: "Why is my voice not heard?"
Surely you are the man who used to say that for an uncertain
truth you could not cast off the baggage of vanity. Behold, there is
now certainty and that burden still weighs upon you. Others have
received wings to liberate their shoulders from the load, others

was a garden attached to our house, which we used as we did the whole house, for the master of the house did not live there. There the tempest in my breast drove me, there where no one would impede the fierce suit which I had brought against myself until it could be settled—in what way you knew but I did not. But there I was, going mad on my way to sanity, dying on my way to life; aware how evil I was, unaware of how much better I was to be in a little while. Therefore, I withdrew into the garden, and Alypius followed close after me. For I was no less in privacy when he was near. And how could he forsake me in such a state? We sat down as far from the house as we could. My mind was frantic, I was boiling with indignation at myself for not going over to your law and your covenant, O my God, where all my bones cried out that I should be, extolling it to the skies. And the way there is not by ship or chariot or on foot. The distance is not as great as I had come from the house to that place where we were now sitting. For to go there and to arrive fully required nothing other than the will to go, but to will strongly and totally, not to turn and twist a half-wounded will this way and that with one part rising up and struggling with the other part that would keep to the earth.

Finally, in the torment of my irresolution, I made many movements with my body which sometimes men want to make and cannot, if either they have not the limbs to make them or if those limbs be bound with cords, weakened by infirmity, or in some way hindered. If I pulled at my hair, beat my forehead, locked my fingers together, if I clasped my knee within my hand, all this I did because I willed to do it. But I might have willed it and not have done it, if the movement of my limbs had not followed the dictates of my will. Therefore, I did many things when the will was not identical with the power; and I did not do that which would have far more pleased me, which soon after, when I should have the will, I should have the power to do because when I willed, I should will it wholly. For there the power was one with the will, and the very willing was the doing. Yet it was not done and the body more easily obeyed the slightest wish of the mind that the limbs should immediately move than my mind obeyed itself so as to carry out its own great will, which could be accomplished simply by willing.

9

How explain this absurdity? What is the cause of it? Let your mercy enlighten me so that I might ask whether the answer lies in the mysterious punishment that has come upon men and in some deeply hidden damage in the sons of Adam. Why this absurdity? And how explain it? The mind commands the body and is immediately obeyed; the mind commands itself and is resisted. The mind commands the hand to move, and the readiness is so great that the commanding is scarcely distinguishable from the doing. Yet the mind is mind whereas the hand is body. The mind commands the mind to will, the mind is itself, but it does not obey. Why this absurdity? And what is its cause? I say that the mind commands itself to will; it would not give the command unless it willed; yet it does not do what it commands. The reason is that it does not wholly will; therefore it does not

wholly command. It commands insofar as it wills, and it dis-
obeys the command insofar as it does not will. The will is commanding itself to be a will, commanding itself, not another. But
it does not wholly give the command; therefore that is not done
which it commanded. For if the will were wholly itself, a unity,
it would not command itself to will because it would already
will. It is therefore no absurdity, partly to will, partly not to will,
but it is only a sickness of soul to be so weighed down by habit
that even when supported by truth it cannot totally rise up. And
so there are two wills in us because neither of them is whole,
and one has what the other lacks.

10

Let them vanish from your sight, O God, as they do vanish, these
vain babblers and seducers of the mind who, because they have
noticed that there are two wills in the act of deliberating, conclude that there are in us two minds of two different natures—
one good, the other evil. They themselves are truly evil when
they believe these evil opinions, and these same men could be
good if they were to realize the truth and consent to the truth so
that your apostle may say to them: "Once upon a time you were
darkness, but now you are light in the Lord" (Eph 5:8). But
these people want to be light not in the Lord but in themselves
when they think that the nature of the soul is what God is. Thus
they have become deeper darkness since they withdrew further
from you in horrid arrogance, from you, the "true Light,
enlightening every man coming into this world" (Jn 1:9). Take

which leads men who have received and are bound by their sacraments to their church; or else they must suppose that in one man there are two evil natures and two evil wills in conflict; and then what they are wont to say will not be true: that there is one good and one evil will. Or else they will have to be converted to the truth and no longer deny that when anyone deliberates, there is just one soul pulled in different directions by different desires.

Let them no longer say, therefore, that when they perceive two conflicting wills in one man the conflict is between two opposing minds of two opposing substances, from two opposing principles, one good, the other evil. For you, O God of truth, refute them and convict them of error, as in the situation where both wills are evil when, for example, a man deliberates whether he should kill a man by poison or by the sword, whether he should seize this or that part of another man's property when he cannot seize both, whether he should squander his money on pleasure or hoard it like a miser, or whether he should go to the games or to the theater if both were to be shown the same day. I add also a third possibility, whether he should rob another's house if the opportunity arose; and I add a fourth, whether he should commit adultery if the chance occurs at the same time. If all these concurred at the same moment and all were equally desired and yet cannot all be simultaneously done, then they truly tear apart the mind among four opposing wills or even more than four when one considers the variety of things which are desirable: Yet the Manichees do not hold such a multitude of different substances. So it is also with good wills. For I ask them whether it is good to take delight in reading the Apostle, and whether it is good to be delighted by the serenity of a Psalm, and good to discuss the Gospel. To each of these they will answer: "It is good." Suppose then these things all equally delight us at the same moment; are not these different wills dividing the heart of man as we deliberate which of these we should choose? All these wills are good, and yet they struggle with one another until one is chosen, and then the whole will, which was divided into many, is unified. So also when eternity delights the higher faculties, and the pleasure of some temporal good holds the lower ones, it is the one same soul which is willing both but not either one with its whole will. And it is therefore torn apart and deeply distressed when truth gives priority to the one way and habit keeps one to the other way.

11

Thus was I heartsick and tortured, accusing myself more bitterly than usual, turning and twisting myself in my chain so that it might be totally broken, for what still held me was so small a thing. But, although small, it still held me. And you, O Lord, stood in the secret places of my soul, by a severe mercy redoubling my lashes of fear and shame, lest I should give way again and lest that small and tender tie which still remained should not be broken but renew its strength and bind me more strongly than ever before. For I was saying within myself, "Behold, let it be done now, let it be done now," and with this word I came to a decision. Now I almost did it, and I did not do it; but neither did I slip back to the beginning but stood still to regain my breath. And again I tried, and I was very nearly there; I was almost touching it and grasping it, and then I was not there; I was not touching it, I was not grasping it. I hesitated to die to death and to live to life; inveterate evil had more power over me than the novelty of good; and as that very moment in which I was to become different drew nearer and nearer, it struck me with more and more horror. But I was not forced back nor turned away but held in suspense between the two.

Trifles of all trifles and vanities of vanities, my former mistresses held me back, plucking at my garment of flesh and softly murmuring: "Are you dismissing us?" and "From this moment shall we never more accompany you?" and "From this moment will you never be allowed to do this or that?" And, my God, what was it, what was it they suggested in those words, "this and that"? In your mercy keep such things from the soul of your servant! How filthy, how sordid were the things they were suggesting! And now I only half heard them nor were they freely contradicting me so openly; it was as if they were muttering behind my back, stealthily jerking my sleeve as I left so that I should turn and look at them. Yet they held me back as I delayed tearing myself away and shaking them off and taking the great step in the direction where I was called. Violence of habit said to me: "Do you think that you can live without them?" But by now it spoke very faintly. In the direction toward which I had turned my face and still trembled to take the final step, I could see the chaste dignity of Continence, serene and calm, cheerful, without wickedness, honestly entreating me to come to her without hesitating, extending her holy hands to receive and embrace me, hands full of multitudes of good examples. With her were many young men and maidens, many youths of all ages, serious widows and women grown old in virginity and in them all Continence herself, not barren but "a fruitful mother of children" (Ps 113:9), her joys by you, O Lord, her spouse. She smiled at me, and there was encouragement in her smile as though she were saying: "Can you not do what these men and women have done? Or do you think that their power is in themselves and not in the Lord their God? The Lord their God gave me to them. Why do you stand upon yourself and therefore not stand at all? Cast yourself upon Him, do not be afraid; He will not withdraw and let you fall; cast yourself fearlessly upon Him. He will receive you and heal you."

And I blushed for shame because I still heard the muttering of those vanities and still hung back hesitantly. And again it was as if she said: "Stop your ears against those unclean members of yours, so that they may be mortified. They tell you of delights, but not of such delights as the law of the Lord your God tells" (Col 3:5). This controversy raging in my heart was about nothing but myself against myself. But Alypius stayed beside me, silently waiting to see how my unusual agitation would end.

12

When from my secret depths my searching thought had dragged up and set before the sight of my heart my total misery, a storm arose within me, bringing with it a great downfall of tears. And so that I might give way to my tears I left Alypius—solitude seemed more suitable for the business of weeping—and withdrew

further so that even his presence might not embarrass me. That is
how I felt, and he realized it. Doubtless I had said something or
other, and he felt the weight of my tears in the sound of my
voice, and so I left him. But he, amazed, remained there where
we were sitting. I flung myself down on the ground somehow
under a fig tree and gave way to tears; they streamed and flooded
from my eyes, "an acceptable sacrifice to you," and I kept saying
to you, perhaps not in these words but with this meaning: "And
you, O Lord, how long? How long, Lord; will you be angry forever? Remember not our former iniquities" (Ps 6:3, 79:5). For I
felt that they still held me fast. In misery I exclaimed: "How
long, how long shall I continue to say: 'tomorrow and tomorrow'? Why not now? Why not this very hour put an end to my
uncleanness?"

This I said, weeping, in the most bitter contrition of my heart.
And suddenly I heard a voice from a neighboring house in a
singing tune saying and often repeating, in the voice of a boy or
girl: "Take and read, take and read." Immediately I stopped weeping, and I began to think intently as to whether the singing of
words like these was part of any children's game, and I could not
remember ever hearing anything like it before. I checked the
force of my tears and rose to my feet, interpreting it as nothing
other than a divine command to open the book and read the first
passage to be found. For I had heard of Anthony that he happened
to enter when the Gospel was being read, and as though the
words were spoken directly to himself he accepted the admonition: "Go, sell all that you have and give to the poor, and you shall

have treasure in heaven, and come, follow me" (Mt 19:21), and by such an oracle he had been immediately converted to you.

So I eagerly returned to that place where Alypius was sitting, for there I had left the book of the Apostle when I stood up. I snatched the book, opened, and read in silence the passage which first met my eye: "Not in rioting and drunkenness, not in chambering and wantonness, not in strife and envying: but put you on the Lord Jesus Christ, and make not provision for the flesh in concupiscence" (Rom 13:13). I did not want to read further, there was no need to. For as soon as I reached the end of this sentence, it was as though my heart was filled with a light of confidence and all the shadows of my doubts were swept away.

Before shutting the book, I put my finger or some other marker in the place; with a calm face I told Alypius what had happened. And he in turn told me what was going on in himself, which I knew nothing about. He asked to see what I had read; I showed it, and he looked further than I had read, and I was unaware of the words which followed. They were these: "Him that is weak in the faith, receive" (Rom 14:1). He applied this to himself and told me so. By this admonition he was strengthened; calmly and without hesitation he joined me in a purpose and resolution so good and so right for his character, which had always been very much better than mine.

Next we go inside to mother and tell her. How she rejoices! We related to her how everything happened; she exulted and gloried and was now blessing you who are able to do above that which we ask or conceive, because she recognized that with regard to me you have given her so much more than she used to beg for when she wept so pitifully before you. For you converted me to you so that I no longer sought a wife nor any other worldly hope. I was now standing on that rule of faith just as so many years before you had shown me to her in a vision. And you had changed her mourning into joy, a joy much richer than she had wanted and much dearer and purer than she looked for by having grandchildren of my flesh.

Book 9

7

The Church of Milan had only lately begun practicing this kind of consolation and exaltation, to the great enthusiasm of the brethren singing together with heart and voice. It was only a year or so ago that Justina, the mother of the boy emperor Valentinian, was persecuting your servant Ambrose on behalf of her own heresy: for she had been led astray by the Arians. The devoted people had remained day and night in the church prepared to die with their bishop, your servant. There my mother, your handmaid, bearing a great part of the trouble and vigil, had lived in prayer. I myself, though not yet warmed by the fire of your spirit, was stirred by the state of excitement and alarm in the city. Then began the practice of singing hymns and Psalms in the manner of the Eastern Churches, lest the people grow faint from sorrow. The custom has continued from that day to this and has been imitated by many, in fact, by almost all of your congregations in other parts of the world.

At that time you revealed to your bishop Ambrose in a vision the place where the bodies of the martyrs Gervasius and Protasius lay hidden. You had for so many years concealed them uncorrupted in your secret treasury from which you might produce them at the proper moment to check the fury of a woman, even though an empress. When they were discovered and unearthed, they were brought with due honor to Ambrose's basilica. Not only were people tormented by unclean spirits cured when these demons acknowledged their presence, but also a certain man who had been blind for many years and as a well-known citizen of Milan asked and was told why the people were shouting with joy. He jumped up and asked his guide to lead him to the place. When he arrived he begged to be allowed to touch with his handkerchief the bier on which were lying the "saints whose death is precious in Your sight" (Ps 115:15). He did this, placed the handkerchief upon his eyes, and immediately his eyes were opened. The news spread abroad. Your praises were fervent and glowing. And Justina was restrained from the insanity of persecution even though her mind was not brought back to the sanity of belief.

Thanks be to you, my God! From where and to where have you led my memory that it should confess to you these great things which I had completely forgotten? Yet even then, "when the odor of the ointments was so sweet smelling" (Cant 1:2–3), I did not "run after you." And so I wept all the more at the singing of your hymns, as one who had once sighed for you and now breathed you in as far as there can be any breath of air in this house of grass (cf. Is 40:6).

8

You, who make "men of kindred minds to dwell in one house" (Ps 67:7), led Evodius, a young man from our town, to join us. He had been in the government service, had been converted to you and baptized before us, had resigned from his official post and became active in your service. We were together, intending to remain together in our devout purpose. We sought for some place where we might more usefully serve you, and therefore we started back to Africa. And when we had come as far as Ostia on the Tiber, my mother died.

I pass over many things because I am in much haste. Accept my confessions and my thanksgiving, O my God, for innumerable things of which I do not speak. But I shall not pass over whatever my soul brings forth about that servant of yours who brought me forth, giving me birth in the flesh to this temporal light, and in her heart to light eternal. Not of her gifts do I speak but of your gifts in her. For she did not make herself nor did she bring herself up. You created her; nor did her father and mother know what kind of being was to come forth from them. The rod of your Christ, the discipline of your only begotten Son, educated her in your fear, in a faithful household worthy to belong to your church. Yet she used to speak not so much of her mother's care in training her as of the care of an elderly woman servant who had carried her father on her back as a baby, as small children are often carried about on the backs of the grown-up girls. Because of this service and on account of her age and excellent behavior, this servant was greatly respected by her master and mistress in this Christian household. Consequently, she had charge of the daughters of the family, one she fulfilled most conscientiously; in restraining the children when necessary she acted sternly and with a holy severity, and in teaching them she manifested sound prudence. For example, except at the times they were fed—and very temperately—at their parents' table, she would not even let them drink water, however thirsty they might be, thus guarding against the formation of a bad habit, saying very sensibly: "Now you are drinking water because you are not allowed to have wine. But when you become married and become mistress of your stores and cellars, water will not be good enough for you, but you will have this habit of drinking." By this advice and by the authority she exercised, she brought under control the greediness from which children suffer and disciplined the girls' thirst to a proper moderation so that they no longer wanted what they ought not to have.

Nevertheless, as your servant [Monica] confided in me, her son, there did come upon my mother an inclination toward wine. For when, as the custom was, she as a good sober girl was told by her parents to go and draw some wine from the barrel, she would hold the cup under the tap, and then before pouring the cup into the decanter, she would sip a little, just wetting her lips, since she did not like the taste and could not take more. Indeed, she did this not out of any craving for wine but rather from the excess of childhood's high spirits, which tend to break loose in ridiculous impulses and which in our childhood years are usually kept under restraint by the sobering influence of elders. And so, adding to that daily drop a little more from day to day—for he "who despises small things shall fall little by little" (Eccl 19:1), she fell into the habit, so that greedily she would gulp down cups almost full of wine. Where then was that wise old woman with her stern prohibition? Was there anything strong enough to deal with a hidden disease unless your healing powers, O Lord, watched over us? Mother, father, and nurses may not be there, but you are there, you who made us, you who call us, you who also use those placed over us to do some good for the salvation of our souls. What did you do then, O my God? How did you cure her? How did you make her healthy? Did you not from another soul bring forth a harsh and cutting taunt, as if bringing forth a surgeon's knife from your secret store, and with one blow amputate that corruption? For a maidservant with whom she usually went to the cellar one day fell into a quarrel with her small mistress when no one else chanced to be about, and hurled at her the most biting insult possible, calling her a drunkard. My mother was pierced to the quick, saw her fault in its true wickedness, and instantly condemned it and gave it up. Just as the flatteries of a friend will pervert, so the insults of an enemy will sometimes correct. Nor do you, O God, reward men for what you do through them but according to what they themselves intended. For that maid being in a temper wanted to hurt her young mistress, not to cure her, for she did it when no one else was there, either because of the time and place where the quarrel started or because she feared that the elders would be angry that she had not mentioned it sooner. But you, O Lord, Ruler of heavenly and earthly things, who turn to your own purposes the very depths of the torrents as they run and order the turbulence of the flow of time, brought health to one soul by means of the unhealthiness of another, showing us that if someone is improved by any word of ours, we must not attribute this to our own power, even if we intended this result to occur.

9

She was educated, therefore, in a modest sober way, being rather made obedient to her parents by you than to you by her parents. And when she reached marriageable age, she was given to a husband whom she served "as her lord" (cf. Eph 5:21). She tried to win him to you, preaching you to him by her behavior in which you had made her beautiful to her husband, reverently lovable and admirable in his sight. So she tolerated his infidelities and never had a jealous scene with her husband about them. She awaited your mercy upon him, that he might grow chaste through faith in you. Although an extremely kind man by nature, he was, in fact, also very hot-tempered. But my mother knew that an angry husband must not be opposed, not in deed or even in word. Only when he had calmed down and had become quiet, when she saw an opportunity, she would explain her actions, if perchance he had been aroused to anger unreasonably. Indeed, there were many wives with much milder husbands who bore the marks of beatings, even in the form of facial disfigurement, and coming together to talk they would complain of their husbands' behavior. Yet my mother, speaking lightly but seriously, warned them that the fault was in their tongues. They had all heard, she said, the marriage contract read out to them, and from that day they should regard it as a legal instrument by which they became servants; so, mindful of their station, they should not set themselves up against their masters. And they were often amazed, knowing how violent a husband she had to live with, that it had never been heard of, nor had there been any evidence to show, that Patricius had ever beaten his wife or that there had been a family quarrel that had lasted as much as a single day. And when her friends asked her intimately how she managed it, she told them her rule, which was as I have just related. Those who followed it found it good and thanked her; those who did not went on being bullied and beaten.

She also won over her mother-in-law by the respect shown her and by unfailing patience and mildness when her mother-in-law had begun by being angry because of the whispers of malicious servants. Her mother-in-law ended by going to her son, telling him of the tales the servants had gossiped about to destroy the family peace between herself and her daughter-in-law, and asking him to punish them for it. So he, out of obedience to his mother and in the interest of household order and peace among the womenfolk, had those servants whose names she had given him beaten. To which she added the promise that anyone must expect a similar reward from her if they tried to please her by speaking ill of her daughter-in-law. None dared after that to do so, and after that they lived together in the sweetness of mutual goodwill.

This great gift also, O my God, my mercy, you gave to your good servant in whose womb you created me, that she showed herself, whenever possible, a peacemaker between people quarreling and minds at discord. She might hear very many bitter things said on both sides, and this outpouring of swelling and undigested malice is very likely to occur when a woman talks to a present friend about an absent enemy; on such occasions hatred is expressed in crude and bitter terms. But my mother would never report to one woman what had been said about her by another except insofar as what had been said might help to reconcile the two. I might consider this a small virtue if I had not had the sad experience of knowing innumerable people who, through some horrible infection of sin, not only tell others who are angry what their enemies said about them in anger, but actually add things which never were said. Whereas ordinary humanity would seem to require not merely restraining from exciting or increasing wrath among men by evil tongues, but that we endeavor to extinguish anger by speaking kindly. This is what my mother did, and you were the master who, deep in the school of her heart, taught her this lesson.

Finally, toward the end of his earthly life, she won her husband over to you, and now that he was a believer she no longer had to lament the things she had to tolerate when he was not yet a believer. She was also the servant of your servants. Whoever knew her praised many things in her, and honored and loved you, because they felt your presence in her heart, through the fruitful evidence of her saintly manner of life. She had been the wife of one husband, had requited her parents, had governed her house piously, was well reported of for good works; she had "brought up her children" as often "travailing in birth of them" as she saw them straying away from you (1 Tm 5:9; Gal 4:19).

Finally, Lord, of all of us—since by your gift we are allowed to speak—who before her death were living together after receiving the grace of baptism, she took as much care as though she were the mother of us all, and served us as though she were the daughter of us all.

10

The day was now approaching on which she was to depart this life—the day you knew though we did not. It came about, as, I believe, by your secret arrangement, that she and I stood alone leaning in a window which looked onto the garden inside the house where we were staying, at Ostia on the Tiber where, apart from the group, we were resting for the sea voyage after the weariness of our long journey by land. There we conversed, she and I alone, very sweetly, and, "forgetting the things that were behind and straining forward to those ahead" (Phil 3:13), we were discussing in the presence of Truth, which you are, what the eternal life of the saints would be like, "which eye has not seen nor ear heard, nor has it entered into the heart of man" (1 Cor 2:9). But with the mouth of our heart we also panted for the supernal streams from your fountain, the fountain of life which is with you (Ps 35:10) so that if some drops of that fountain, according to our capacity, were to be sprinkled over us, we might somehow be able to think of such high matters.

And our discourse arrived at this point, that the greatest pleasure of the bodily senses, in the brightest corporeal light whatsoever, seemed to us not worthy of comparison with the joy of that eternal life, unworthy of being even mentioned. Then with our affections burning still more strongly toward the Selfsame, we advanced step by step through the various levels of bodily things, up to the sky itself, from which the sun and moon and stars shine upon this earth. And higher still we ascended, by thinking inwardly and speaking and marveling at your works, and we came to our own minds and transcended them to reach that region of unfailing abundance where you feed Israel forever on the food of truth (Ez 34:13). There, life is wisdom by whom all these things come into being, both those which have been and those which will be. And wisdom itself is not made; it is as it has ever been, and so it shall be forever: Indeed, "has ever been" and "shall be forever" do not pertain to it, but it simply is, for it is eternal; whereas "to have been" and "to be going to be" are not eternal. And while we were speaking and panting for wisdom, we did with the whole impulse of the heart slightly touch it. We sighed and left behind "the first fruits of the Spirit" (Rom 8:23), which were bound there, and returned to the sound of our own tongue, where the spoken word has both beginning and ending. How is it like your word, our Lord, "remaining ageless in Itself and renewing all things" (Ws 7:27)? We said therefore: If to any man the uproar of the flesh grew silent, silent the images of earth and sea and air; and if the heavens also grew silent and the very soul grew silent to itself, and by not thinking of self ascended beyond self; if all dreams and imagined revelations grew silent, and granted me superabundantly, for I see you as His servant to the contempt of all worldly happiness. What am I doing here?"

11

What I answered to this I do not clearly remember; within five days or not much longer she fell into a fever. And in that sickness she one day fainted away and for the moment lost consciousness. We ran to her, but she quickly regained consciousness, and seeing my brother and me standing by her, she said to us, as though seeking an answer to some question, "Where am I?" Then gazing intently upon us as we stood speechless in our grief, she said: "Bury your mother here." I was silent and restrained my weeping; but my brother said something about hoping that she would have the good fortune to die in her own country and not in a foreign land. But when she heard this, she looked anxious and gave him a reproachful look because he still relished earthly things. Then she looked into my face and said: "See how he talks." Soon she said to both of us: "You may lay this body of mine anywhere: Do not worry at all about that. All I ask you is this: that wherever you may be, you will remember me at the altar of the Lord." And when she had expressed this wish in such words as she could, she fell silent as the agony of her sickness grew stronger upon her.

But as I considered your gifts, O invisible God, which you have placed into the hearts of your faithful and which have produced such wonderful fruit, I rejoiced and gave thanks to you, recalling that I knew how worried and anxious she had always been about the question of her burial. She had already provided herself and prepared a tomb close to that of her husband. Since they had lived together in such harmony, she had wished—so little is the human mind capable of grasping things divine—that it should be granted her as an addition to her happiness and to have it spoken of among men, that after her pilgrimage across the sea the earthly part of both man and wife should lie covered under the same earth. Just when this vain desire began to leave her heart through the plenitude of your goodness, I did not know; but I was pleased and surprised that it had now vanished, although in that conversation of ours together in the window, when she said: "What am I still doing here?" she had shown no desire to die in her own country. Furthermore, I later heard that when we were at Ostia, she spoke one day to some of my friends, as a mother speaking to her children, of the contempt of this life and of the good of death. I was not there at the time. They marveled at such strength of a woman—but it was you who had given it to her— and inquired whether she was not afraid to leave her body so far from her own city. "Nothing," she said, "is far from God, and I do not fear that he will not know at the end of the world from what place He is to raise me up." And so on the ninth day of her illness, in the fifty-sixth year of life and the thirty-third of mine, that religious and holy soul was released from the body.

12

I closed her eyes; and an immense wave of sorrow flooded my heart and would have overflowed in tears. But my eyes under the mind's strong constraint seemed to pump that fountain dry, and in that struggle it was agony for me. Then as soon as she had breathed her last, the boy Adeodatus broke out in lamentation until, constrained by all of us, he grew silent. But in this very deed the childish element in me, which was breaking out in tears, was checked and silenced by the manlier voice of my mind. For we felt that it was not appropriate that her funeral should be marked with moaning and weeping and lamentation, because these are the ways people grieve for an utter wretchedness in death or a kind of total extinction. But she had not died miserably nor did she wholly die. Of this we had good reason to be certain from the evidence of her way of living and from her "unfeigned faith" (1 Tm 1:5).

What was it then that grieved my heart so deeply except the freshness of the wound, in finding the custom I had so loved of living with her suddenly snapped short? I rejoiced in the testimony she gave me in the very last days of her illness when, as I was doing what service I could for her, she spoke so affectionately to me, calling me her good and dutiful son. With such great love she told me that she had never once heard me say a word to her that was hard or bitter. And yet, my God, who made us, what comparison was there between the honor I showed her and the service she rendered me?

Because I had now lost the great comfort of her, my soul was wounded and my very life torn asunder, for it had been one life made up of hers and mine together. So when the boy was quieted from weeping, Evodius took up the Psalter and began to chant—

with the whole house making the responses—the Psalm "Mercy and judgment I will sing to You, O Lord" (Ps 101:1). And when it was known what we were doing, many brethren and religious women gathered. And while those whose function it was made arrangements for the burial, I with some of my friends who thought I should not be left alone found another part of the house where we could properly be, and there I spoke to them on such subjects as I thought appropriate for the occasion. So I was using truth as a kind of balm to relieve my torment, a torment known to you but unknown to the others. They listened closely to me and thought that I lacked all feeling of grief. But in your ears, where none could hear me, I rebuked the tenderness of my feeling and suppressed the flow of guilt. It yielded a little, then gathered strength and again swept back on me, though not with any outburst of tears or change of facial expression. But I well knew what I was crushing down in my heart. I was ashamed that those human feelings could be so strong in me—though it belongs to the due order and the lot of our earthly condition that these things should be—and I felt a new grief at my grief and so was afflicted with a twofold sorrow.

When the body was carried to the grave, we went and returned without tears. During the prayers we poured forth to you when the sacrifice of our redemption was offered for her—while the body, as customary there, lay by the grave before it was actually buried—during those prayers I did not weep. Yet all that day I was heavy with hidden grief, and in my troubled mind I begged you, as best I could, to heal my sorrow; but you did not, impressing, I think, upon my memory by this one experience how strong is the bond of all custom even when that soul now feeds upon no deceiving word. It seemed to me that I should go to bathe myself because I had heard that the word for bath—which the Greeks called *balneum*—was derived from the Greek *balaneion* because it drives anxiety from the mind. And this also I confess to your mercy, O Father of orphans, that I bathed and was the same man after as before. The bitterness of grief had not sweated out of my heart. Then I fell asleep and awakened to find that my grief was much relieved. And as I lay alone in bed I remembered those true verses of your Ambrose: for it is you who are

> Creator Thou of everything
> Director of the circling poles
> Clothing the day in lovely light
> Giving night the grace of sleep
> That peace may fall on loosened limbs
> To make them strong for work again
> To raise and soothe the tired mind
> And free the anxious from their care.

Then little by little I began to recover my former feelings about your handmaid, her devout and holy behavior in regard to you, her saintly kindness and benevolence toward us, of which I was suddenly deprived. And I found solace in weeping in your sight both about her and for her, about myself and for myself. So I allowed the tears which I had been holding back to fall, and I let them flow as they would, making them a pillow for my heart, and my heart rested on them, since only your ears were there, not those of some man who would have scornfully misunderstood my tears. And now, O Lord, I am confessing this to you in writing. Anyone who cares can read what I have written and interpret it as he likes, and if he finds it is sinful that I wept during this small portion of an hour for my mother, now dead and lost to my sight, who had wept so many years for me that I should live ever in your sight, let him not despise me but rather, if he is a man of great charity, let him weep for my sins to you, the Father of all the brethren of your Christ.

Book 10

7

What then do I love when I love my God? Who is He above the summit of my soul? Through this very soul of mine I shall ascend to Him. I shall go beyond my life-force by which I cling to the body and fill its frame with life. Not by that force do I find my God: If so, "the horses and mules which lack understanding" (Ps 32:9) could find him since their bodies also live by that same force. But there is another force, not only that by which I not only give life, but give sensation to my flesh, which the Lord fashioned for me, commanding the eye not to hear and the ear not to see, but giving me the eye to see by and the ear to hear by, assigning to each of the other senses its own particular duty and function. Through these senses, with all their different functions, I act as one soul. I shall also go beyond this force, for this also the horse and the mule have: They also sense through the body.

and all odors through the nostrils; all tastes through the mouth; and by the sensation of the whole body we derive our impression of what is hard or soft, of whatever is hot or cold, or whatever is smooth or rugged, heavy or light, whether from outside or inside the body itself. All these sensations are received into the great harbor of memory with its many secret and indefinable recesses, to be produced when need requires, each coming in by its own entry and there stored up. Yet the things themselves do not enter, but the images of things perceived are there ready at hand for thought to recall.

Who can say how these things are formed? Yet it is clear by which senses they entered and were stored up. For even while I remain in darkness and silence, I can, if I wish, call forth colors in my memory and note the difference between black and white and any other colors I like, and when I reflect on the images drawn in by my eyes, sounds do not come running in to disturb them, though they also are in my memory, stored up, as it were, in a separate compartment. For I can summon forth sounds also, if I wish, and they are immediately present; with no movement of tongue or vocal chords I sing as much as I please, nor do those images of color, although present in the memory, intrude and interrupt when I summon something from that other storehouse containing impressions brought in by the ear. And so I call forth as I like all other things brought in and stored up by the other senses. I can discern the difference between the smell of lilies and violets though I am actually smelling nothing at the time, and I prefer honey to sweet wine, something smooth to something rough merely by memory, using neither the sense of taste nor that of touch.

This I do within, in that huge court of my memory. There I

have available to me the sky, the earth, the sea, and all those things in them which I have been able to perceive—apart from what I have forgotten. There also I encounter myself; I recall myself—what, when, and where I have done something; and how I felt at the time. There are all things I remember to have experienced myself or to have heard from others. From the same storehouse also I can summon forth pictures of things which have either happened to me or are believed on the basis of experience. I can myself weave them into the context of the past; and from these I infer future actions and events and hopes, and on these again I contemplate as if they were present. "I shall do this and that," I say to myself in this deep recess of my mind, full of the images of so many and such great things, "and this or that follows." "Oh, if only this or that could happen!" or "May God prevent this or that!" So I say to myself, and while I am speaking, the images of all the things that I am saying are present to my mind, all from this same treasury of my memory: in fact, if the images were not there, I would not be able to speak of these things at all.

How great is the power of memory, how exceedingly great, O God; a vast and unlimited interior; who has plumbed its depths? Yet this is a power of my mind and belongs to my nature; I myself do not grasp all that I am. Is then the mind too narrow to hold itself so that the questions arise: Where is this which belongs to it, and it cannot grasp? Is it outside itself and not inside? How then does it not grasp itself? Faced with all this, great wonder arises in me, astonishment seizes me. And men go abroad marveling at the heights of mountains, at the huge waves of the sea, at the broad courses of the rivers, the vastness of the ocean, the circular motions of the stars, and yet do not notice themselves and see nothing marvelous in the fact that when I was mentioning all these things, I was not observing them with my eyes. Yet I could not have spoken of them unless these mountains and waves and rivers and stars, which I have seen, and the ocean of which I have heard, had been visible to me inside, in my memory, and with precisely the same great intervals and proportions as if I were really seeing them outside myself. Yet by the act of seeing I did not draw them into myself; not they themselves but only their images are within me, and I know by what bodily sense each impression came to me.

27

Late have I loved you, O Beauty, so ancient and so new, late have I loved you! And behold, you were within me and I was outside, and there I sought for you, and in my deformity I rushed head-long into the well-formed things that you have made. You were with me, and I was not with you. Those outer beauties held me far from you, yet if they had not been in you, they would not have existed at all. You called and cried out to me and broke open my deafness: you shone forth upon me, and you scattered my blindness: you breathed fragrance, and I drew in my breath, and I now pant for you: I tasted, and I hunger and thirst; you touched me, and I burned for your peace.

28

When I with my whole self shall cleave to you, there will no longer be for me sorrow or labor; wholly alive will my life be, being wholly filled with you. Those whom you fill you raise up, and now, since I am not yet full of you, I am a burden to myself. Pleasures of this life in which I should find sorrow conflict with the sorrows of this life in which I should rejoice, and on which side stands the victory I do not know. Woe is me, O Lord, have pity on me: My evil sorrows conflict with my good joys, and on which side stands the victory I do not know: Woe is me, O Lord, have mercy on me! Woe is me! Look, I am not concealing my wounds: You are the physician and I am ill; you are merciful, I need mercy. "Is not human life on earth a trial" (Jb 7:1)? Who wishes to have troubles and difficulties? These you order us to tolerate, not to love. No one loves what he tolerates, even though he loves to tolerate. For however greatly he rejoices in his toleration, he would yet prefer to have nothing to tolerate. In adversity I desire prosperity, in prosperity I fear adversity. What middle place is there between these two where human life is not all trial? All the prosperities of this world are caused again and again—by the fear of adversity and by the corruption of joy. And the adversities of this world are cursed once, twice, and thrice—by the desire for prosperity, by the very bitterness of adversity itself, and by the fear that it may break down our toleration. Is not then human life on earth a trial without intermission?

43

But the true Mediator, whom in your secret mercy you have manifested to men and have sent him so that they, by his example, might learn humility, that "Mediator between God and men, the Man Christ Jesus" (1 Tm 2:5), appeared between mortal sinners and the immortal Just One: mortal with men, just with God; so that, because the wages of justice is life and peace, He might by a justice conjoined with God make void the death of sinners justified by him; for He was willing to allow that death be common to Him and to them. He was revealed to the holy men of old so that they might be saved through faith in His coming passion as we are saved through faith in His passion which has come to pass. For insofar as He is man, He is mediator; but insofar as He is the Word, He is not midway between God and man; for He is equal to God, both God with God, and together one God.

How much you have loved us, Good Father, who "did not spare your only Son, but delivered Him up for us" (Rom 8:32), the ungodly! How you have loved us, for whom "He who thought it not robbery to be equal with you was made subject even to the death of the cross" (Phil 2:6, 8). He "alone free among the dead, having power to lay down His life, and power to take it up again" (Ps 88:5): For us He was to you both victor and victim (Jn 10:18), and victor because victim: For us He was to you both priest and sacrifice, and priest because sacrifice: and He made us sons to you instead of slaves by being born of you and becoming your slave. Deservedly, then, my hope in Him is strong, that "you will heal all my infirmities" (Ps 102:3) through Him who "sits at your right hand making intercession for us" (Rom 8:34); otherwise I should despair. For many and great are my infirmities, yes, many and great; but your medicine is still greater. We could have thought that your word was far removed from any union with man and thus despaired of ourselves, unless it had been "made flesh and dwelt amongst us" (Jn 1:14).

Terrified by my sins and the burden of my misery, I pondered in my heart about a plan to fly to the wilderness. But you forbade me and strengthened me, saying: "Therefore Christ died for all, that they who live may now no longer live unto themselves, but unto Him who died for them" (2 Cor 5:15). See, Lord, "I cast my care upon you" (Ps 55:22) that I may live and "consider the wondrous things of Your law" (Ps 119:8). You know my unskillfulness and my weakness; teach me and heal me. He, your only Son, "in whom are hid all the treasures of wisdom and knowledge" (Col 2:3), has redeemed me with His blood. "Let not the proud speak evil of me" (Ps 119:22), for I meditate on the price of my redemption. I eat it and drink it and give it to others. And being poor myself, I desire to be satisfied by it among those who "eat and are satisfied, and they shall praise the Lord who seek Him" (Ps 31:16).

THE HAPPY LIFE

This is the first dialogue begun by Augustine in the villa at Cassiciacum near Milan, where he lived from the autumn of 386 while preparing for baptism to be received after Lent in 387. Here Monica, her son Adeodatus, his brother Navigius, two cousins (Lastidianus and Rusticus), two students (Licentius and Trygetius), and the friend Alypius prayed, studied, and held philosophical discussions, which were recorded by a stenographer.

This dialogue opens with a comparison of the search for Truth to a dangerous voyage with pride as the enormous mountain barring the way to the harbor and threatening shipwreck. In Augustine's case, Manichaean rationalism had been the obstacle that was finally removed by his discovery of the spiritual and sacred nature of the soul through reading the Platonic books and listening to the sermons of Ambrose.

The discussants agree that happiness is more directly related to the soul's condition than to bodily well-being and wealth since the latter can be lost whereas the God loved by the virtuous is an abiding reality. In his Retractations 1.2 Augustine corrects the impression he gave in 2.14 of this dialogue that perfect happiness can be had in this life. The happiness condition of the soul is Wisdom. Although Augustine, his friends, and all people are merely seekers of Truth, they can be united within themselves to the Source of truth or happiness when they overcome the moral obstacles to the sincere desire for God. The reference to the soul's being in direct contact with God is a conviction derived from Neoplatonic teaching. Plotinus taught that the spiritual icon is always in immediate contact with its exemplar, the higher intelligible that is its source. In this earliest use of the soul as the image of God, Augustine is holding that the intelligible source from which the soul comes and with which it remains in intellectual contact is the Eternal Truth or God Himself. This develops into his theory of illumination and his demonstration of God's existence in the dialogue On Free Choice of the Will.

Most gracious and renowned Theodore, I am not certain that I would be speaking rashly in saying that if it were our own will and a course directed by reason which lead us to the port of philosophy, whence one proceeds to the land and Kingdom of the happy life, a much smaller number of men would have arrived there than actually have, although now also, as we see, only few arrive there and infrequently. For since God or nature or necessity or our own will or some assortment of these or all of them together have cast us into this world (for the matter is very obscure but is proposed so that you can shed light on it) as into a stormy sea, accidentally and indiscriminately, as it were, what man would know in what direction to struggle or where to return unless some tempest, to the foolish apparently bad luck, should push us unwilling, resisting, unwitting, and off our course, upon the land we most of all longed to reach?

2

Therefore, it seems to me that there are three classes of seafarers, whom philosophy can include. The first class consists of those who, on reaching the age of reason, with little effort and a lazy stroke of the oars, shove off a short distance and establish themselves in a state of tranquillity, in which they set up a striking sign of their work, such as it is, so that as many citizens as possible, enticed by this sign, may try to join them.

Now the second class, quite different from the former, consists of those who, misled by the beguiling appearance of the sea, choose to proceed out into the middle of the deep and venture to sail far away from their native land, which they often forget. If a wind from the stern, which they believe favorable, has sometimes mysteriously accompanied them, they enter, elated and rejoicing, into the deep waters of misfortune because everywhere a most deceptive serenity of pleasure and honors continually entices them. What, indeed, should they desire more than some upset in those affairs by which they are pleasurably ensnared and, if that does not suffice, a completely devastating tempest and a gale blowing in the opposite direction to bring them, despite their weeping and wailing, to sound and genuine joys? Many of this class, however, if they have not yet sailed too far, are brought back by adversities that are not so serious. These are the men who, when the miserable tragedies of their fortunes or the anxious cares of their vain business affairs have driven them, as it were (as if they had nothing else to do), to the books of learned and wise men, somehow awaken in the harbor from which they cannot be lured by any promises of that deceitfully smiling sea.

There is a third class between these two who, either on the very threshold of youth or after being rocked long and far upon the sea, look back to certain beacons and recall their dearly beloved native land although they are now surrounded by waves. Either they set forth on a direct course for their homeland again, neither deceived nor delayed, or more often, wandering in the midst of a fog or intently watching the sinking stars or held by some alluring charm, they neglect good opportunities for sailing, and, off course too long, they are sometimes even in danger. They are also often driven by some adversity of shifting fortune like a tempest, as it were, opposing their efforts, back home and to a most welcome rest.

3

To the distress, moreover, of all who in any way are traveling to the land of the happy life, a large mountain bars the way to the port itself, causing the passage to be extremely narrow for incoming sailors. This mountain must be very seriously feared and carefully avoided. For it is so splendid and clothed in such deceptive light that it disguises itself as a dwelling place to those arriving and not yet landed, promising to quench their desire for the happy life itself. It often also attracts men from the harbor itself to come out, often captivating them by delight in its sheer height, whence they like to look down upon others. They often warn newcomers not to be deceived by hidden rocks or to think that it is easy to climb them, and in a most helpful way, they show newcomers where, because of the nearness of the land, they may without danger enter. And so to newcomers envious of their vainglory they show a place of security.

Does reason teach those approaching and entering upon philosophy that they should fear any mountain more than the proud pursuit of empty glory? For within it there is nothing substantial or solid, and, with a cracking of the ground-crust beneath, it collapses and swallows up those walking above, puffed up with themselves, and, as they tumble headlong into darkness, it withdraws from them the gleaming dwelling place just barely seen.

4

Since this is the case, please learn, my good Theodore—for to you alone I look for what I desire and at your great ability I always marvel—please learn which of the three classes of men has given me to you, in what place I myself seem to be, and what kind of help I confidently expect of you. At the age of nineteen, when in the school of rhetoric I came upon Cicero's book *Hortensius*, I was inflamed with such enthusiasm for philosophy that I thought of devoting myself to it immediately.

But there was no lack of mist to confuse my course, and for some time, I confess, I followed stars falling into the ocean, and so I was led astray. For a kind of childish superstition caused me to cringe before inquiry itself, and when having become self-reliant, I dispelled that mist and persuaded myself to submit to those who teach rather than to those who command, I met men by whom the light seen by the eyes was beheld as that which was an object of highest and even divine veneration. I did not agree, but I thought they were concealing within those veils some important secret, which at some time they would divulge.

But when I shook off those men and escaped, especially after I had crossed this sea, for some time the Academics held the tiller of my ship as, surrounded by waves, it battled all winds. Then I came to this land. Here I have learned to know the North Star to which I entrusted myself.

Often I noticed in the sermons of our priest, and sometimes in yours, that when there was consideration of God or of the soul, which is nearest to God, there was to be no thought at all of anything corporeal. The enticements of a woman and of fame kept holding me back, I confess, from flying immediately into philosophy's embrace, so that not until I had satisfied my desire for these did I—and this has been granted only to the most fortunate few—under full sail and with all oars pulling make that harbor quickly and there find rest. But having read a few books of Plotinus, of whom I understand that you are a zealous student, and having compared them, as well as I could, with the authority of those who have handed down the divine mysteries, I was so inflamed that I would have cast off all those anchors holding me if my esteem for certain men had not restrained me. What then remained except that a storm which seemed ill luck should come to my rescue as I hesitated, occupied with unnecessary cares? And so such a violent chest ailment seized me that, unable to bear the burden of my profession, by which perhaps I was sailing to the Sirens, I threw everything overboard and brought my ship, battered and weary, to the desired resting place.

5

Therefore, you see the philosophy in which, as in a port, I am now sailing. But even the port itself lies wide open; although its great size presents less danger, yet it does not entirely exclude error. For I am not at all aware to what part of the land I should move—that part which alone is really happy—and how I should reach it. For what do I hold as firm, since up to now the question about the soul is still wavering and uncertain? Wherefore I entreat you through your virtue, through your kindness, through the spiritual bond and fellowship between us, that you extend your helping right hand, for this means that you love me and that you may believe that I in turn love you and hold you dear. If I obtain this request, I shall arrive very easily and with slight effort at that happy life in which I presume you already share.

But that you may know what I am doing and how I am gathering my dear ones at the port, and from this more completely understand my mind—for I cannot find any other signs by which to reveal myself to you—I thought that one of my discussions which seemed to me more religious in character and especially worthy of your fame should be addressed to you and dedicated to your name.

This is surely most appropriate for together we have inquired concerning the happy life, and I know nothing else which should rather be called a gift of God. I am not frightened by your eloquence, for whatever I love I cannot fear, although I may not attain it; much less am I frightened by the height of your good fortune. For, although it is great, it is truly secondary in your consideration because it puts in second place the very ones whom it dominates. But now please listen to what I say.

6

My birthday fell on the Ides of November. After a breakfast light enough not to in any way impede our thinking, I invited all who were living together, not only that day, but every day, to meet at the bathing quarters, a sequestered place appropriate for the season. The following were present—for I do not hesitate to present them to your kindness, though only by name: first of all, our mother, to whose merit I believe is due all that I am; Navigius, my brother; Trygetius and Licentius, fellow-citizens and students of mine; and I do not want to omit Lastidianus and Rusticus, my cousins. Although they had no grammatical training, I thought that their very common sense was necessary to the discussion which I was trying to lead. Also with us was Adeodatus, my son, the youngest of all, whose ability, if I am not blinded by love, promises something great. When I had gained their attention, I began thus.

7

"Does it seem clear to you that we are composed of soul and body?" Although all the others agreed, Navigius replied that he did not know.

"Do you know nothing at all," I said to him, "or is this to be counted as just one of the things of which you are ignorant?"

He replied, "I don't think I am ignorant about everything."

"Can you tell us some of the things which you know?"

"I can," he said.

"Unless it is difficult," I continued, "mention something."

Since he hesitated, I suggested, "You know at least that you are alive?"

"Yes," he declared.

"You know therefore that you have life, since no one can live except by life."

"This also," he said, "I know."

"You also know that you have a body?"

He assented.

"Then you already know that you consist of body and life."

"I know that much, but I am uncertain whether there are only these two."

"Therefore you are not in doubt," I said, "about these two, body and soul, but you are uncertain whether there is something else needed to make up and complete a human being."

"Yes," he replied.

"We shall later inquire into, if we can, what this something else is," I said. "I now ask this question of all, since we all agree that man cannot exist without body or soul: On account of which of those do we seek food?"

"On account of the body," said Licentius.

But the others hesitated now on this side, now on that, how food can seem necessary for the body when it is sought on account of life, and life pertains only to the soul. Then I asked, "Does it seem to you that food pertains to that part which we see grow and become stronger through food?" All agreed except Trygetius, who objected, "Why haven't I grown in proportion to my great appetite?"

"All bodies have a measure fixed by nature," I replied, "which they cannot exceed. Yet they would be smaller than this measure if they were deprived of food. We notice this very readily in regard to domestic cattle, and no one doubts that the bodies of all living things grow thin when denied food."

"Grow thin," replied Licentius, "not grow small."

"That is enough for my purpose," I said. "Indeed, the question is whether food pertains to the body. But it does pertain to the body since, deprived of food, the body becomes emaciated." All agreed that this was the case.

8

"What, then, of the soul?" I continued. "Has it nourishment of its own? Or does it seem to you that knowledge is its food?"

"Clearly," said Mother, "I believe that the soul has no other nourishment than knowledge and the understanding of things."

When Trygetius showed that he doubted this statement, she continued, "Today haven't you yourself taught us whence and where the soul is fed? For you said that only after breakfast had been going on for some time you noticed what bowl we were using, because you were thinking about something else, and yet your hand and mouth were not unused during the first part of the meal. Where, then, was your soul at the time you paid no attention to what you were eating? In this way, believe me, and by such repasts the soul is nourished, that is, on its thoughts and concerns, if through them it can learn something."

When they were murmuring their doubts on this point, I said, "Do you not concede that the souls of learned men are much fuller and in their own way much greater, as it were, than the souls of the uneducated?"

They said that this was obvious.

"Therefore we rightly say that the souls of those untrained in any studies and who have not become possessed of skills and arts are, as it were, hungry and famished."

"I think their souls are also full," said Trygetius, "but full of vices and worthlessness."

"This very worthlessness," I said, "believe me, is a kind of barrenness and hunger of souls. For just as a body denied food is often afflicted with sickness and scabs, illnesses which point to hunger, so the souls of the uneducated are also filled with diseases which reveal their malnutrition. Indeed, the ancients wanted it known that the very word *nequitia* [worthlessness], the mother of all vices, is derived from *nequicquam* [to no purpose], that is, from that which is nothing. The opposite virtue of this vice is called *frugalitas* [worth]. Therefore, as the latter word is from *frux* [fruit], which in turn is from *fructus* [productive of enjoyment], because of a kind of fruitfulness of souls, so the former word *nequitia* [worthlessness] takes its name from barrenness, that is, from that which is nothing. For *nihil* [nothing] is whatever is in a state of flux, and which disintegrates, dissolves, and, as it were, is always perishing (*perit*). For this reason we also say that such men are *perditi* [lost beyond recovery].

"But whatever endures, if it continues, if it is always the same, is something positive and real, as is virtue. A great and most beautiful part of virtue is called *temperentia* [moderation] and *frugalitas* [worth]. But if this is so obscure that you cannot now see it, you will certainly admit that if the souls of the uneducated are themselves also full, then there are two kinds of food for the soul just as there are two kinds of food for the body: one, wholesome and helpful, the other, unwholesome and harmful.

9

"Since this is the case, I think that on my birthday, insofar as we are agreed that there are two components of man, body and soul, I should serve a somewhat more festive meal not only for our bodies but also for our souls. And if you are hungry, I shall tell you what this meal will be. For if, disdaining the food and against your will, I try to feed you, in vain shall I exert myself and ought rather to pray that you will enjoy such feasts more than those for the body. This will be so if your souls are healthy; for sick souls, as we see in respect to physical illness, refuse their food and spit it out." All declared by their facial expressions as well as by their spoken agreement that they were ready to take and eagerly eat whatever I had prepared.

10

And so, beginning again, I said: "We want to be happy, do we not?" As soon as I said this, they unanimously assented.

"Does a man who does not have what he wants," I said, "seem to you to be happy?" They said no. "Well, is everyone who has what he wants happy?"

Then Mother said: "If he wants and possesses good things, he is happy; but if he wants evil things, although he possesses them, he is unhappy."

Smiling at her, I exclaimed cheerfully: "You have truly gained the mastery of the very stronghold of philosophy, Mother. For without doubt only for lack of words you did not elaborate on this subject as did Tullius [Cicero], whose words will follow. For in the *Hortensius*, the book he wrote on the praise and defense of philosophy, he said: 'But see, surely not the philosophers but all given to argument say that those who live just as they wish are happy.' This is definitely false; for to want what is not appropriate is the worst of all miseries. It is not so miserable not to get what you want as to want to get what you ought not. Wickedness of will brings to everyone greater evil than good fortune brings good."

At these words, she so exclaimed that we, entirely oblivious of her sex, believed that some great man was with us. Meanwhile I understood, as well as possible, from what source those words came and how divine was the source.

Then Licentius said, "You must tell us what a person ought to wish for in order to be happy, and what kind of things he must desire."

"Invite me on your birthday," I answered, "if you will be so kind. I shall gladly receive whatever you serve. In this spirit I beg that you dine with me today and that you do not insist on having what has perhaps not been prepared."

When he regretted his excitement, although it was modest and proper, I asked, "Are we therefore in agreement on this point, that no one who does not have what he wants can be happy and not everyone who has what he wants is happy?"

They granted this.

11

"Well, then," I continued, "do you grant that everyone who is not happy is miserable?"

They did not doubt that.

"Everyone, therefore," I went on, "who does not have what he wants is miserable."

This was accepted by all.

"How, then, should a man provide for himself so that he may be happy?" I asked. "Perhaps this will also be supplied for our feast so that the eagerness of Licentius may not go unheeded for, in my opinion, he ought to obtain that which one possesses wherever one wants it."

They said that was evident.

"Then it must always be something enduring, not depending on chance, not subject to misfortunes, for we cannot have whatever is mortal and transient whenever we wish it and as long as we wish to have it."

All except Trygetius assented. "There are many fortunate people who possess abundantly and lavishly these very same fragile possessions which are subject to misfortunes and yet give pleasure to this life, nor do they lack any of the things they want."

I responded: "Does it seem to you that he who fears is happy?"

"It does not seem so," he replied.

"Then if anyone can lose what he loves, is it possible for him not to fear?"

"It is not possible."

"But these things which depend on chance can be lost. Therefore, whoever loves and possesses such things can in no way be happy."

He did not continue arguing. But at this point Mother said, "Even if he is assured that he cannot lose all these things, yet with such things he will not be satisfied. Therefore, he is unhappy because he is always needy."

"Suppose," I said, "enriched and overflowing with all these things, he should limit his desire and contentedly, fittingly, pleasantly enjoy what he has, would he not seem happy to you?"

"Then he is not happy," she answered, "because of those things, but because of the moderation of his own mind."

"Very good," I cried. "No other answer should have been made to this question, and certainly no other by you. Hence, in no way do we doubt that if anyone has decided to be happy, he must secure for himself what is permanent, what no misfortune, however grave, can snatch away."

"To this," said Trygetius, "we already fully consent."

"Does God seem to be eternal and abiding forever?" I asked.

"This is so certain," said Licentius, "that there the question is superfluous." All the others with pious devotion assented.

"Therefore," I said, "whoever possesses God is happy."

12

While with joy they were most willingly accepting this statement, I added: "There is nothing, therefore, I think, which we must now inquire about other than what kind of man possesses God, for certainly he will be happy. On this I would like to know your opinion."

Whereupon Licentius said: "He who lives well possesses God."

Trygetius suggested: "He possesses God who does what God wills to be done."

Lastidianus concurred in this statement. But the boy, youngest of all, said: "He possesses God who does not have an unclean spirit."

Mother approved all the opinions but especially the last.

Navigius kept silence. When I asked him what he thought, he answered that the last statement pleased him.

Nor did it seem proper not to learn the opinion of Rusticus on such an important topic. It seems to me that he was tongue-tied by shyness rather than deliberately silent. He agreed with Trygetius.

13

Then I said: "I now have all your views on this obviously important topic beyond which it is not necessary to inquire nor can any conclusion be reached even if we continue to investigate it very calmly and earnestly, as we began to do. Since the investigation today would be tiring, and since even souls suffer from overabundance in their feasts, if they indulge in them greedily and to excess (for they get a kind of indigestion which should be guarded against for the sake of health no less than against that very hunger we have discussed), we shall better resume this question tomorrow when hungry, if that is satisfactory to you. Meanwhile, I should like to have you munch freely on a tidbit which has suddenly come into your host's mind as something that must be served, and which unless I am wrong, is—like those dishes usually served last—concocted and seasoned, as it were, with scholastic honey."

Having heard this, all reached forward, as it were, toward a dish being offered, and they insisted that I immediately tell them just what it was.

"Well," I said, "do you think that the whole business of discussion which we have undertaken with the Academics has been completed?"

Having heard that name, the three to whom this matter was familiar eagerly arose and, with outstretched hands, as it were, in the usual manner, helped the host to serve, showing with whatever words they could that there was nothing they could be more pleased to hear.

14

Then I proposed the matter this way: "If it is obvious that a man who does not have what he wants is not happy—which reason demonstrated a short time ago—but no one seeks what he does not want to find, and the Academics are always seeking truth, hence want to find truth, therefore wanting the power to find truth—but they do not find it—it follows that they do not have what they want, and from that it also follows that they are not happy. But no one is wise unless he is happy: Therefore there is no wise Academic."

Whereupon they suddenly exclaimed as if hastily grasping the whole thing. But Licentius, listening more carefully and cautiously, feared assent and added: "I joined you in that snack since the conclusion moved me to exclamation. But I shall swallow no more of this and shall save my share for Alypius; for either he will relish it together with me or he will advise me why it should not be touched."

"Navigius with his troublesome spleen ought to be more careful with sweets," I said.

He laughingly replied, "Such things will certainly cure me, for the dish you set before us, somehow concocted and spiced, is, as Cicero says of Hymettic honey, bitterly sweet and does not bloat my stomach. Hence, after a taste of it, I gladly swallow it all to the extent of my capacity. For I do not see how that conclusion can be refuted."

"In no way can it be refuted," said Trygetius, "and so I rejoice that long ago I began to oppose them. For impelled by natural impulse or, to speak more truly, by the grace of God, although I knew not how they were to be refuted, nevertheless I greatly opposed them."

15

Here Licentius interrupted. "As for me, I do not yet abandon them."

"Then," asked Trygetius, "you disagree with us?"

"Does any one of you," he replied, "disagree with Alypius?"

"I have no doubt," I said, "that if Alypius were here he would assent to this conclusion. For he could not hold such an absurd opinion: either that a man who lacks such a great good for the soul and a good ardently desired seems happy; or that those men do not wish to find the truth; or that he who is not happy is wise. For the dish you fear to taste is concocted of these ingredients, as it were, honey, meal, and nuts."

"Would he yield to this miserable bait for children," he replied, "forsaking the wonderfully rich argumentation of the Academics, which by its abundance will either overwhelm this short and insignificant discussion of ours or extend it?"

"As if, indeed, we were seeking something long, especially against Alypius, for he himself would in no small way prove from his own body that those small ingredients provide vigor and utility. But you, who have chosen to depend on the authority of someone absent, which of these statements do you not approve? Is it the statement that he who does not have what he wants is not happy? Or do you deny that those men wish to find and possess the truth they eagerly seek? Or does it seem to you a wise man is not happy?"

"Certainly he who does not have what he wants is happy," he said, laughing almost peevishly.

When I requested that this statement be written down, he exclaimed, "I didn't say that."

When again I motioned that it be written down, he admitted, "I did say it."

And I ordered once and for all that every word should be committed to writing. Thus I kept the youth on their toes between modesty and constancy.

16

But while with these words I was jokingly urging him to eat his morsel, so to speak, I noticed that the others who had not heard this part of the discussion and were eager to know what was going on so pleasantly just between the two of us were looking at us without smiling. And to me they seemed especially like those who—as often happens—when they dine with very greedy and hungry guests, refrain from taking food quickly either through consideration or modesty.

And since it was I who had done the inviting—and you have shown how to play the role of a great man (that of a real man, to explain it fully) and how to remain the host even at feasts of this kind—the inequality and discrepancy at our table disturbed me. I smiled at Mother. Bidding them draw from her supply, as it were, what they needed, she said: "Now tell us who these Academics are and what purpose they have in mind."

When I had explained to her briefly and so clearly that none of the group might leave ignorant, she asserted: "Those men are epileptics" (this term is used colloquially among us to designate those suffering from "falling sickness"). At the same time she stood up and left.

And at this point, having ended our discussion, we all departed, happy and laughing.

17

The next day when again we all assembled after breakfast in the same place but somewhat later than the previous day, I said, "You have come late to the feast. I don't think this has occurred from indigestion yesterday but because, aware of the small number of courses, you thought it best not to come so early since you would finish eating quickly. For you believed that there could not be many leftovers when on the very day of the birthday celebration only a small amount of food was served. Perhaps you believed correctly. But I am with you in not knowing what has been prepared for you.

"For there is another who never ceases to supply not only all meals to all men but also especially such feasts as these, but we frequently cease eating either because of weakness, or satiety, or business. He is the one who, dwelling in men, makes them happy as, unless I am mistaken, we piously and firmly agreed yesterday. For since reason proved that he who possesses God is happy, and none of you opposed this conclusion, the question was asked: Who, in your opinion, possessed God. On this question, if I remember well, three opinions were expressed. Some held that whoever does what God wants possesses God; but others said that whoever lives well possesses God; but to the rest it seemed that God is in those in whom there is not present what is called an unclean spirit.

18

"But perhaps you all have one and the same feeling, though expressed in different words. For if we consider the first two statements, namely, everyone who lives well does what God wills, and everyone who does what God wills lives well, living well is nothing other than doing whatever pleases God, unless it seems otherwise to you."

They agreed.

"Truly that third opinion should be considered a little more carefully because, according to the rites of the most pure Mysteries, the term *unclean spirit*, as far as I know, is usually interpreted in two ways: either a spirit which invades a soul from outside and confuses the senses and causes a sort of frenzy in people, and those qualified to dismiss such a spirit are said to lay hands upon or exorcise it—that is, to drive it out by adjuring it in the name of God—or else, every impure soul, that is, one defiled through vices and sins, is called an unclean spirit.

"Therefore, I ask you, my boy, you who expressed that opinion perhaps from a somewhat calmer and purer spirit, who do you think does not have an unclean spirit, that one who does not have a demon whereby men are usually made mad, or that one who has cleansed his soul from all vices and sins?"

"It seems to me," he said, "that he who lives purely does not have an unclean spirit."

"But," I continued, "whom do you call pure, he who does not sin at all, or only the one who refrains from illicit intercourse?"

"How can he be pure," he said, "who refrains only from illicit intercourse and does not cease to defile himself with other sins? That man who attends to God and devotes himself solely to Him is truly pure."

When I had ordered that the boy's words be written down just as he had uttered them, I then said: "Such a man necessarily lives well, and whoever lives well has to be such a man, unless you think otherwise."

Along with the others he agreed.

"Therefore the opinion expressed here is unanimous," I said.

19

"But I shall question you a little on this point: whether God wishes man to seek Him."

They conceded this.

"I likewise ask whether we can say that a man who seeks God lives wickedly."

"In no way," they answered.

"Also tell me your answer to this third question: Can an unclean spirit seek God?"

They denied this possibility, although Navigius, at first hesitating, later yielded to the opinion of the others.

"If, then, a man who seeks God does what God wills, he lives well and has no unclean spirit. But he who seeks God does not yet possess Him. Therefore, not everyone who lives well or who does what God wills or who has no unclean spirit should be said forthwith to possess God."

At this point when all the others, deceived by their own concessions, were laughing at themselves, Mother, who had been dumbfounded for a time, requested me to unravel and clarify the logical knot I had been compelled to present. When I did this, she objected, "But no one who has not sought God can reach God."

"Very good point," I said, "but he who still seeks has not yet reached God, yet he is already living well. Therefore, not everyone who lives well possesses God."

"It seems to me," she replied, "that there is no one who does not have God, but those who live well have God favorably inclined, while those who live wickedly have Him inclined unfavorably."

"Yesterday, then, we were wrong," I said, "when we agreed that he who possesses God is happy if it is the case that everyone possesses God and yet not everyone is happy."

"Add, then, the phrase 'favorably inclined,'" she replied.

20

"At least," I went on, "are we agreed on this: that a man who has God favorably inclined toward him is happy?"

"I should like to agree," objected Navigius, "but I fear the case of the man still seeking, especially lest you conclude that the Academic is happy who in yesterday's discussion was designated by the term *epileptic* (*caducarius* [one who falls] in vulgar and bad Latin, but most aptly, so it seemed to me).

"For I cannot say that God is unfavorable to a man who seeks Him. But if it is wrong to say that, He will be favorably inclined, and whoever has God favorably inclined is happy, therefore he who seeks will be happy. But anyone seeking does not yet possess what he wants; hence that man who has not what he wants will be happy, a conclusion which yesterday seemed absurd to all of us, whereupon we believed that we had dissipated the confusions of the Academics. Hence Licentius will now exult over us, and like a wise physician he will warn that those sweets I rashly accepted against my health are exacting this punishment from me."

21

At this point, when even Mother had smiled, Trygetius said, "I do not absolutely agree that God is opposed to anyone toward whom He is not favorably inclined, but I think there is some middle position."

I questioned him: "Do you agree that a man in a middle position, that is, a man toward whom God is neither favorably nor unfavorably inclined, in some way possesses God?"

When he hesitated at this, Mother said, "It is one thing to possess God; it is another not to be without God."

"Which, then," I asked, "is better: to possess God or not to be without Him?"

"As far as I can understand," she replied, "this is my opinion: Whoever lives well possesses God, but as favorably inclined; whoever lives wickedly possesses God, but as unfavorably inclined; but whoever is still seeking Him and has not yet found Him has God as neither favorably nor unfavorably inclined but is not without God."

"Is this also the opinion of all of you?" I asked. They said that it was.

"Please tell me," I said, "doesn't it seem to you that God is favorably inclined to a man whom he favors?"

They admitted this.

"Then," I asked, "does not God favor a man who seeks Him?"

They replied that He does favor him.

"Therefore," I said, "whoever seeks God has God favorably inclined toward him, and everyone who has God favorably inclined toward him is happy; hence, he who is seeking is happy; but he who seeks does not yet possess what he wants; consequently, he who does not have what he wants will be happy."

"Surely," objected Mother, "a man who does not have what he wants does not seem happy to me."

"Therefore," I said, "not everyone who has God favorably inclined toward him is happy."

"If reasoning requires this," she replied, "I cannot deny it."

"Therefore, this will be the distinction," I said; "everyone who has already found God has God favorably inclined and is happy, but anyone seeking God has God favorably inclined but is not yet happy; however, whoever by vices and sins alienates himself from God not only is not happy but does not even live with God favorably inclined toward him."

22

When this pleased all, I said, "Very well, but I still fear that what we previously conceded may disturb you: namely, whoever is not happy is miserable. It will follow that a man is miserable who has God favorable to him since—as he said—he still seeks God and therefore is not yet happy. Or, to quote Tullius, 'shall we call the owners of large estates throughout the world "rich" and call the possessors of all virtues "poor"?' But consider this: whether, just as it is true that every needy person is miserable, it is likewise true that every miserable one is needy. For thus it will be true that there is no other misery than neediness, an opinion which as soon as it is expressed, you notice that I commend. But it would be tedious to inquire into it today. So I ask you, lest you be satiated, to assemble please at this table again tomorrow."

When all had said that they would gladly do so, we arose.

23

On the third day of our discussion the morning mist, which was keeping us in the bathing quarters, lifted and a very bright afternoon returned. Hence it seemed good to descend to the small meadow nearby. When all were seated wherever they wanted, the rest of the discussion proceeded thus: "Almost everything," I said, "which I wanted you to concede when I questioned you, I have and retain. Therefore, today so that we can at last interrupt our feast by a space of days, there will be nothing or not much, in my opinion, to which you must reply. Mother stated that unhappiness is nothing but neediness, and we agreed that persons who are needy are unhappy. But whether all who are unhappy are also needy is an important question which yesterday we could not answer. But if reason demonstrates that this is the case, it will be most adequately discovered who is happy, for it will be the person who is not in need. For everyone who is not unhappy is happy.

"Therefore whoever is without needs is happy, if what we call 'need' (*egestatem*) constitutes 'unhappiness' (*miseriam*)."

24

"Well, then," said Trygetius, "because it is clear that everyone in need is unhappy, cannot the conclusion now be drawn that anyone not in need is happy? For I remember we agreed that there was no middle position between happiness and unhappiness."

"Does there seem to you to be any middle position between life and death, or is not every man either living or dead?" I asked.

"I admit," he said, "that there is no middle position in that; but why this question?"

"Because," I said, "I believe that you will also admit this: whoever has been buried for a year is dead."

He did not deny this.

"Well, is everyone who has not been buried for a year alive?"

"It does not follow," he answered.

"Then," said I, "neither does it follow that if everyone who is in need is unhappy, everyone not in need is happy, although there is no middle position between happy and unhappy, just as between life and death."

25

Since some of them only very slowly understood this argument, explaining and presenting as well as I could with words suitable for comprehension, I said: "Therefore no one doubts that everyone in need is unhappy, nor are we alarmed that even wise men need certain things for their bodies. The soul in which the happy life is placed does not need these things. For the soul itself is complete, and no soul, being complete, needs anything; and while it takes whatever seems necessary for the body if it is there, if it is not there, the lack of such things will not crush it. Every wise man is strong, and the strong man entertains no fear. For every wise man fears neither bodily death nor sufferings. For the banishment, prevention, or delay of such pains he would need all those things of which he is capable of being in want. Yet he does not fail to use them well if they are there. For very true is that aphorism, 'It is foolish to suffer what you can avoid.' Therefore, he will avoid death and pain as far as it is possible and fitting so that, if he does not avoid them, he will not be unhappy when they occur but because he refused to avoid them when it was possible, behavior which is a clear sign of folly. And so whoever does not avoid these things will be unhappy not from enduring them but from folly.

"But if he cannot avoid them, although his behavior has been careful and proper, they will not make him unhappy. Indeed, this aphorism of the comic poet is no less true: 'Since what you wish for is impossible, better wish for what is possible.' How will he be unhappy to whom nothing happens against his will, since he cannot want anything which he sees he cannot get? For he has his will directed toward very definite things so that, whatever he does, he does only according to some precept of virtue or divine law of wisdom, and in no way can these be taken from him.

26

"Now, then, consider whether everyone who is unhappy is also in need. To admit that is rather difficult in view of the fact that for many living amidst great abundance of fortuitous wealth and who have at their disposal all things so that at their nod they can have whatever their whims dictate, that life is indeed pleasant and easy.

"But let us imagine such a person as Tullius says that Orata was. For who would readily say that Orata suffered from need, he who was the richest, the most charming, the most pampered of men, who lacked nothing with respect to pleasure, popularity, and good sound health? For he had an abundance of lucrative land and genial friends, as many as he wanted, and all these he used very advantageously for his physical welfare, and, briefly, a prosperous outcome followed his every plan and desire. Some of you, perhaps, will suggest that he wanted to have more than he had. Does he seem to you to have been in need?"

"Even if I agreed," objected Licentius, "that he wanted nothing more, which I would scarcely admit in the case of an unwise man, he must have feared (for he was, it is said, a man of no small intelligence) that he would lose all with one adverse stroke of fortune. For it was not very difficult to realize that all such things, however great they may be, were subject to chance."

Then I, smiling, said to him, "Licentius, you see how this most fortunate man was kept by the keenness of his intellect from the happy life. For the keener he was, the more he realized that he could lose all those things. He was crushed by this fear and fully confirmed that commonplace: 'The faithless man is wise in his own folly.'"

27

When he and the others had laughed at this, I continued, "Let us, however, examine this question more carefully because, although he was afraid, he was not in need, and this raises a question. For to be in need consists in not having, not in fear of losing what you have. But this man was unhappy because he was afraid, although he was not in need. Not everyone, therefore, who is unhappy is in need."

Even Mother, whose position I was defending, along with the others approved this. Still a little in doubt, she said: "I still do not know nor do I yet clearly understand how unhappiness can be separated from need and need from unhappiness. For even this man who was rich in money and land and, as you say, desired nothing more, nevertheless because he feared to lose his wealth, he lacked wisdom. Therefore, would we not say that he was in need if he lacked silver and money? Shall we not say that he was in need when he lacked wisdom?"

When all cried out in admiration and I myself was very excited and pleased because it was she in particular who had stated what I had learned with great trouble from the books of the philosophers and had planned to bring forth last, I asked, "Do you all see that a great difference exists between many and varied doctrines and a soul wholly attentive to God? For whence come those words which we admire unless from Him?"

Here Licentius joyfully exclaimed: "Surely nothing truer, nothing more divine could be said. For no need is greater and more unhappy than lack of wisdom, and whoever does not lack wisdom cannot lack anything at all."

28

"A needy mind, then," I said, "is nothing else but folly. For folly is the opposite of wisdom, and opposite in the way that death is the opposite of life and that the happy life is the opposite of the unhappy life, that is, with no middle position. Just as every man not happy is unhappy, and every man not dead is alive, so it is obvious that every man not foolish is wise."

"From this we also may see that Sergius Orata was unhappy, not so much because he feared losing those gifts of fortune, but because he was foolish. So it is that he would have been more unhappy if he had not at all feared for those things, unstable and perishable as they were, which he considered good. For he would have felt more secure through mental laziness than through the protection gained by courage, and by his greater folly he would have been steeped more deeply in unhappiness. Now if everyone who is foolish suffers great need and everyone possessing wisdom lacks nothing, it follows that folly is a need. And as everyone who is foolish is unhappy, so everyone unhappy is foolish. Therefore, just as all need is to be considered unhappiness, so all unhappiness is to be considered need."

29

When Trygetius said that he did not very well understand this conclusion, I said, "What did our reasoning convince us of?"

"That a man who lacks wisdom is in need," he answered.

"What, then, is being in need?" I asked.

"Not to have wisdom," he replied.

"What is not to have wisdom?" I went on.

When on this point he was silent, I asked, "Is not this to have folly?"

"It is," he assented.

"To have need, then, is nothing but to have folly," I said. "From this it necessarily follows that need (*egestas*) is merely designated by another name when it is called folly (*stultia*), although I am unable to explain how we shall say, 'He has need' or 'He has folly.' For this is like saying that some place lacking light has darkness—which is nothing but lacking light. Now darkness does not come and go, as it were, but lack of light is itself identical with darkness, just as lack of clothing is identical with being naked. When clothing is put on, nakedness does not depart as if it were a mobile thing. So we say that someone has need in the sense in which we say he has nakedness, for 'need' is an expression for not having. Accordingly, to explain my meaning as well as possible, when we say 'He has need,' this is identical with saying 'He has not-having.' And so if it has been shown that folly is a genuine, definite lack, let us see whether the question we just raised has now been answered. For among us there was some doubt whether we meant anything other than need when we used the word 'unhappiness.' But we have now given a reason why folly is correctly called need. Just as every man, therefore, who is foolish is unhappy, and every man who is unhappy is foolish, so we must concede not only that everyone who is in need is unhappy but also that everyone who is unhappy is in need. But if we conclude from the fact that everyone foolish is unhappy and everyone unhappy is foolish that folly is unhappiness, why do we not conclude from the fact that whoever is in need is unhappy and whoever is unhappy is in need that unhappiness is nothing but need?"

30

When they all admitted that this was so, I said: "This now follows, that we should see who is not in need, for he will be wise and happy. 'Folly' (*stultia*) is need and a synonym for 'need,' and this word usually signifies a kind of sterility and lack. Notice, therefore, how either all the words of the ancients or, at least, what is apparent here, certain words were created to designate what is very necessary to know. For you already concede that everyone who is foolish is in need and everyone in need is foolish. I believe you will also agree that a soul without wisdom is vicious and that all the imperfections of the soul are included in the one term 'folly.' Moreover, on the first day of our discussion, we said that *nequitia* [worthlessness] was so called because it is *nequicquam* [not anything] and is the opposite of *frugalitas* [worth], which was derived from *frux* [fruit]. Therefore in these two opposites, namely, fruitfulness and unfruitfulness, these two qualities seem to stand out: 'to be' [*esse*] and 'not to be' [*non esse*]. But what do we think to be the opposite of need, which is the question at hand?"

When they somewhat hesitated here, Trygetius said, "If I should speak about riches, I see that poverty is their opposite."

"That is certainly clear," I said, "for poverty and need are usually taken as one and the same thing. But another word must be discovered so that at least one positive synonym may not be lacking, for although there are adequate negative terms like 'poverty' [*paupertas*] and 'need,' the term 'riches' [*divitiae*] is the only positive term opposed to them. Nothing is more absurd than the lack of a term as counterpart of 'need.'"

"'Fullness,'" suggested Licentius, "if I may say so, seems to me the correct opposite of 'need.'"

31

"Later we shall inquire perhaps more carefully about the word," I said, "for this is not the main concern in our search for truth. For although Sallust, that most learned weigher of words, uses 'opulence' (*opulentia*) as the opposite of 'need,' nevertheless I accept your 'fullness' (*plenitudo*). For here, at least, we shall be freed from fear of grammarians or from fear of being chastised for the careless use of words by those who gave us the use of their property."

When they had laughed at this, I said, "Therefore, since I did not plan while you were intent on God to disregard your minds as I would oracles, so to speak, let us see what this word signifies, for I think that no word is more suited to the truth. Fullness and need, then, are opposites. But likewise here also, as in unfruitfulness and fruitfulness, these two qualities appear, namely, 'to be' and 'not to be,' and if need is identical with folly, fullness will be wisdom. Justly have many said that worth is indeed the matter of all the virtues. And agreeing with them, Tullius also says in one of his orations before the people, 'Let everyone decide as he wishes, but I consider worth, that is, moderation and restraint, the greatest virtue.' Surely a very scholarly and fitting statement, for he considered *frux*, that is, what we are calling *esse*, the opposite of *non esse*. But because of ordinary language in which *frugalitas* is commonly identified with *parsimonia* [thrift], he clarifies what he means by two following words, that is, adding *modestia* [moderation] and *temperantia* [restraint]. Let us examine more closely these two words.

32

"*Modestia* is said to come from *modus* [measure] and *temperantia* from *temperies* [a proper blend]. Now where there is measure and proper blend, there is nothing too much or too little. Therefore, that word 'fullness,' which we proposed as the opposite of 'need,' is a much better choice than 'abundance' [*abundantia*]. For by abundance is understood affluence and a kind of overflow of something present in superabundance. If this happens in excess, measure is lacking, and the thing which is in excess lacks measure. Therefore, need is not alien to superabundance itself, but too much and too little are alien to measure. If you also analyze the word *opulentia* itself, you will discover that it contains only measure, for the word is clearly derived from *ops* [wealth]. But how does that which is too much help, since too much is often more inconvenient than too little? Therefore, whatever is either too little or too much, because it lacks measure, is subject to need. Therefore the measure of the mind is wisdom. For it is not to be denied that wisdom is the opposite of folly, and folly is need. But fullness is the opposite of need. Therefore, wisdom is fullness, and in fullness there is measure; therefore, the measure for the mind is in wisdom. Hence that excellent and rightly famous aphorism: 'This is the most useful principle in life: nothing too much.'"

33

"At the outset of yesterday's discussion, however, we said that if we found that unhappiness was nothing but need, we would concede that a man who is not in need is happy. Now this has been discovered to be true. Hence to be happy is nothing but not to be in need, that is, to be wise. But if you seek what wisdom is, reason has already explained and declared this as far as presently possible. For wisdom is nothing but the measure of the soul, that is, that by which the mind is liberated so that it neither runs over into too much nor falls short of fullness. For there is a running over into luxuries, tyrannies, acts of pride, and other such things whereby the souls of unrestrained and unhappy men think they get for themselves pleasure and power. But there is a falling short of fullness through baseness, fear, sorrow, passion, and other things, of whatever kind, whereby unhappy men even admit that they are unhappy. But when one contemplates the wisdom that has been discovered, and to use this boy's words, devotes himself to it and, unmoved by any vanity, does not turn to the deceptions of idols, whose authority, when embraced, is wont to lead one away from God and plunge one into destruction, one fears no lack of restraint and therefore no need and, accordingly, no unhappiness. Whoever therefore has his own measure, that is, wisdom, is happy."

34

"But what should be called wisdom except the wisdom of God? Moreover, we have received on divine authority that the Son of God is none other than the wisdom of God, and the Son of God is truly God. Therefore, whoever possesses God is happy, which we all agreed upon at the outset of this symposium. But what do you think wisdom is except truth? For this was also said: 'I am the truth.' Now truth exists through some supreme measure from which it proceeds and unto which it is converted when perfected. Moreover, no other measure is imposed on the supreme measure, for if the supreme measure is a measure through the highest measure, it is the very measure through itself. But it is necessary that the highest measure also be a true measure. Therefore, just as truth is begotten of measure, so measure is known by truth. Therefore truth has never been without measure, and measure has never been without truth. Who is the Son of God? 'Truth,' it has been said. Who is it who has no father? Who other than the Supreme Measure? Whoever, then, has arrived at the Supreme Measure through truth is happy. For souls this is to possess God, that is, to enjoy God. For although other things are possessed by God, they do not possess God.

35

"Moreover, a certain admonition which incites us to remember God, to seek Him and, having banished pride, to thirst after Him, comes forth to us from the source of truth. That secret sun pours that beaming light into our inward eyes. To this source belongs all the truth which we speak even when we still fear, on account of our weak or recently opened eyes, to turn boldly toward it and to gaze upon it in its entirety. And this light appears to be nothing other than God who is perfect and without any fault. For there we find every perfection in its entirety, and at the same time He is the most omnipotent God. But as long as we seek and are not yet satisfied by the source itself— and to use that word, by fullness [plenitude]—let us confess that we have not yet attained our measure and therefore, although we already have God's help, nevertheless we are not yet wise and happy. This, therefore, is the complete satisfaction of souls, that is, the happy life: to know precisely and perfectly Him through whom you are led into the truth, the nature of the truth you enjoy, and the bond that connects you with the Supreme Measure! These three show to those who understand the one God, the one Substance, excluding the variety of all vain and superstitious images."

Whereupon Mother, having recalled words which dwelt firmly in her memory, as if awakening to her faith, uttered this verse of our priest: "'Assist, O Trinity, those who pray,'" and added, "This is unmistakably the happy life, a life which is perfect, toward which it must be presumed that, hastening, we can be led by a well-founded faith, joyful hope, and ardent love."

36

"Therefore," I said, "since measure itself advises us to spread our colloquium over a certain number of days, to the best of my ability, I give thanks to the supreme and true God, the Father, the Master, the Liberator of souls, then to you who, although cordially invited, have generously heaped gifts upon me. You have contributed so much to our conversation that I

ON THE TRINITY

On the Trinity was undertaken by Augustine without his being asked to write it by others. A strong heresy of the fourth century was that of Arius, who attempted to be utterly faithful to Christianity as monotheism by teaching the "natural" subordination of the Son to the Father. He spoke of the Son and the Spirit as creatures.

Yet Augustine's treatise On the Trinity is theological rather than polemical, an instance of faith seeking understanding. It is, moreover, a work that manifests the intimate connection between theology and spirituality. He begins in Book I with the teaching of the Trinity derived from Scripture and articulated in the Council of Nicaea as well as by the Cappadocian Fathers: Basil of Caesarea, Gregory of Nyssa, Gregory of Nazianzus:

> Father, Son, and Holy Spirit constitute a divine unity of one and the same substance in an indivisible equality. Therefore they are not three gods but one God; although the Father has begotten the Son and, therefore, He who is Father is not the Son; and the Son was begotten by the Father and, therefore, He who is the Son is not the Father; and the Holy Spirit is neither the Father nor the Son, but only the Spirit of the Father and the Son, and He Himself is also co-equal with the Father and the Son and belongs to the unity of the Trinity.

In the first few books Augustine explains that scriptural statements regarding the Son as less than the Father refer to the Son in the "form of a servant" when made flesh. He then discusses the "Missions" of Son and Spirit in the world. The Son's great Mission was the Incarnation. He became flesh to manifest God's love in order to cure us from pride, heal us from the wounds of sin, and unify us as His Mystical Body. The Holy Spirit's main Mission was made evident at Pentecost, and the Spirit continues in the Church to vivify it with truth and charity.

After interpreting Scripture, Augustine uses reason to show that the distinction between substantive and relative terms can safeguard the divine simplicity and the unity in nature of the three divine Persons. Person, according to Augustine, is not an adequate term to use of any one of the three-in-one God because it usually denotes a substance. In the Trinitarian context it is used to say that as Son (person), that is, related to the Father, the Son is not the Father (person), that is, Begetter of the Son. It is therefore more accurate to say: God is Father, Son, and Spirit than to say God is three Persons.

In Book 8, Augustine enters into himself to study the soul in order the better to understand the Trinity. As image of God, humanity must also include a unity in trinity, and Augustine first finds this in love, which is impossible without a lover, a beloved, and a loving. God has been revealed as Love, and this demands plurality. The way to knowledge of God is through love, not any kind of love, but charity, the gift of God. Augustine was greatly impressed by the Johannine Gospel and Epistles, where we learn that God becomes present where there is love.

But we cannot remain at the level of the image. The Christian is called to ascend from the image to the contemplation of the Divine Reality. In Book 14, parts of which are presented here, we find the culmination of the spiritual life to be the soul's participation in Divine Wisdom, wherein God Himself is the object of the mind's memory, understanding, and will. If God has made us toward Himself, then our hearts will be restless until they rest in Him. Therefore the spiritual life embraces both time and eternity. The one reality that is present here below and will forever continue is that of charity, which requires the presence of God and our awareness of God as Love. Through the gift of charity, or Grace, God unites people together, and as a temple or sacred city they are a dwelling place of the Trinity-God in whose likeness they grow in the measure of their love.

—MARY T. CLARK

Book Fourteen

Chapter 12

There is an uncreated Being who has made all other beings great and small, certainly more excellent than everything He made, and thus also more excellent than the rational and intellectual being which we have been discussing, namely, the mind of man, made to the image of its Creator. And the Being more excellent than all others is God. Indeed, He is "not far from any one of us," as the Apostle says, adding, "for in him we live and move and have our being" (Acts 17:27f). Were this said in a material sense, we could understand it of our material world: for in it also, in respect to our body, we live and move and are. The text should be taken, however, in a more excellent and also invisible and intelligible way, namely, with respect to the mind that has been made to His image.

In fact, what is there that is not in Him of whom Holy Scripture says: "For from Him and through Him and in Him are all things" (Rom 11:36)? If all things are in Him, in whom, except in Him in whom they are, can the living live or the moving move? Yet all men are not with Him in the sense in which He says "I am always with you" (Ps 73:23). Nor is He with all things in the sense in which we say, "The Lord be with you." The great misery of man, therefore, is not to be with Him without whom he cannot exist. Unquestionably, man is never without Him in whom man is; but if a man does not remember Him, does not understand Him or love Him, he is not with Him. But complete forgetfulness makes it impossible even to be reminded of what we have forgotten.

Chapter 13

To clarify this, let us take an example from the visible world. A man whom you fail to recognize says: "You know me"; and to remind you, he says where, when, and how you met him. After he gives all the clues to revive the memory of him and you still do not recognize him, this means that you have forgotten him so completely that there is no trace of your former knowledge and you can only believe his assurance that you once knew him, or you do not believe him if he does not seem credible. Clearly, however, if you do remember, you are returning to your memory, discovering therein what was not completely forgotten and erased. Now let us return to what led us to draw a parallel with human encounters. In the ninth Psalm we read the words: "Let the sinners be turned to hell, all the nations which forget God" (Ps 9:18). Or again, in the twenty-second: "All the ends of the earth shall be reminded, and shall turn unto the Lord" (Ps 22:27). Therefore, these nations had not so forgotten God that they could not remember Him when reminded. By forgetting God, which was like forgetting their own life, they had been turned toward death, that is, toward hell. But, when reminded, they are turned to the Lord, revived through the remembrance of their proper life of which forgetfulness had deprived them. We may compare the text of the ninety-fourth Psalm: "Understand now, you unwise among the people: return finally, you fools, to wisdom. He who planted the ear, shall he not hear?" and so forth (Ps 94:8f.). The words are addressed to those who have spoken vainly concerning God by not understanding Him.

Chapter 14

There are many more testimonies in Scripture to the love of God, and in this the other two mental elements are logically implied since no one can love what he does not remember nor love that which he does not know. This is the best-known and the principal commandment: "You shall love the Lord your God" (Dt 6:5). The human mind is naturally constituted so as never to be without the memory, the understanding, and the love of itself. But inasmuch as the desire to harm accompanies hatred of a man, it is reasonable to say that a man's mind hates itself when it is harmful to itself. When the mind does not know that what it wants is harmful, its ill will to itself is unconscious, but in wanting what is harmful, it is willing evil to itself. So it is written: "He who loves iniquity hates his own soul" (Ps 11:5). Consequently, the man who knows how to love himself properly loves God; whereas the man who does not love God, even if he retains a natural self-love, may properly be said to hate himself when he acts against his own good, acting as an enemy to himself. That is certainly a frightful delusion whereby, with all men desiring their own profit, so many do what brings ruin to them. Vergil describes a similar distemper in dumb animals in these words:

and love of itself, and thus is justified the above quotation: "Though man walks in an image, yet is he vainly disquieted: he heaps up treasures, and knows not for whom he shall gather them" (Book XIV.4.ii). Why does he heap up treasures except that his strength has forsaken him—the strength in which by possessing God he needed nothing else? And why does he not know for whom he shall gather them but because the light of his eyes is not with him? So he is unable to see what truth would tell him: "You fool, this night they require your soul of you; then whose shall those things be which you have provided?" (Lk 12:20).

Yet man, although fallen, still "walks in an image," and his mind retains a memory, an understanding, and love of himself; so that if it were made clear to him that he cannot have both, and a choice offered of one of the two with loss of the other—either his stored-up treasures or his mind—there is no one so mindless as to prefer treasures to mind. Treasures very often can conquer the mind; but the mind not conquered by treasures is able to live an easier and more unobstructed life without them. Who can possess treasures except through the mind? A child born to the greatest wealth, though owner of all that he legally possesses, as long as his mind is dormant possesses nothing. How, therefore, can anything be possessed by one who has lost his mind? It is in fact needless to suggest that any man, facing the choice, should prefer the loss of treasures to the loss of mind. No one could prefer treasures or even find them of comparable value to his bodily eyes, which give possession not as of gold to a few fortunate ones but of the wide heaven to every man. By using the bodily eyes, everyone possesses whatever he delights in seeing. Who then would not choose, if he could not keep both and must be deprived of one, to lose his treasures rather than his eyes? Likewise, if asked whether he would rather lose eyes or mind, every "mind" must see that he would rather keep his mind and lose his eyes. For without the bodily eyes the mind is still human, but the bodily eyes without the mind are the eyes of a beast—who would not prefer to be a blind man than a seeing beast?

My purpose in this argument was to convince even those slower in comprehension among those reading or hearing what I have written of the strength of the mind's self-love even when it is weak and erring through the misguided love and pursuit of inferior things. Now it would not be able to love itself if it were entirely ignorant of itself—that is, it did not remember itself—and did not understand itself. Such power it has by virtue of God's image within it that it is able to cleave to Him whose image it is. It has been placed in that order of reality, not a spatial order, where there is none above it but God.

And when its cleaving to Him has become absolute, it will be one spirit with Him: witness the words of the Apostle, "He that is joined to the Lord is one spirit" (1 Cor 6:17), by drawing near, in order to participate in that being, truth, and bliss without this adding anything to His own being, truth, and bliss. Joined to that Being in perfect happiness, the mind will live within that Being a changeless life, enjoying the changeless vision of all it beholds. Then, as Holy Scripture promises, its desire will be satisfied "with good things" (Ps 103:5), with unchanging goods, with the very

Trinity itself, its God whose image it is. And that nothing may ever injure it, it will abide "in the secret place of his countenance" (Ps 31:20), so full of His abundance that sin can never again delight it. But here and now when the mind sees itself, what it sees is not unchangeable.

Chapter 15

Of this it can have no doubt since it is miserable and longs for happiness. Only because it is able to change is it able to hope that happiness is possible for it. For if it were unchangeable, it could change neither from bliss to misery nor from misery to bliss. Under an omnipotent and good Lord nothing but its own sin and its Lord's justice could have made it miserable. Nothing but its own merit and its Lord's rewarding will make it blissful; and even its merit is a grace from Him whose reward will also be its bliss. For the justice it has lost and now lacks it cannot give itself. That justice was received at creation and was lost inevitably by its own sinning. Therefore it must receive justice in order to deserve to receive bliss. To a mind inclining toward pride in a good considered its own doing, the Apostle asserts this truth: "What hast thou that thou hast not received? And if thou hast received, why does thou boast as if thou hast not received it?"

But when rightly remembering its Lord, it receives His spirit, becoming fully aware of the truth learned from the inner Teacher, that it can ascend only by the affection He freely gives, just as it could have fallen only by its own voluntary failure. In fact, it has no memory of its own happiness, for that was once and is no longer, and the mind has entirely forgotten it, so that no reminder can bring it back. But it believes in the Scriptures of its God that are worthy of faith and written by His Prophet, when they tell of a paradisal happiness and relate the account of man's original good and evil yet remembers the Lord its God. For He always is—neither has He been and is not, nor is He and has not been, but just as He never will not be, so never was He not. And He is everywhere in His totality; so that in Him the mind lives and moves and has its being, and consequently can remember Him. Not that it recollects that it had known Him in Adam, or anywhere else before this bodily life, or at its first making and settling in this body. Of none of these things has it any memory at all; all of them are buried in forgetfulness. But it is reminded that it should turn to the Lord as to that light by which it was somehow touched even when it was turned away from Him. Hence arises the ability even in the godless to think of eternity and to assign praise and blame rightly in the sphere of human morality.

By what norms do they make such judgments if not by those in which they recognize how every man should live, although their own lives are not an example of this? Where do they see such norms? Not in their own nature: for the mind unquestionably sees them, whereas their minds are admittedly changeable; but the changelessness of these norms is evident to all who have the power to see them. Nor does it see them in any state of their own mind; for the norms are norms of justice, and their minds are admittedly unjust.

Where are the norms written, whereby what is just is recognized by the unjust man, and in which he sees that he ought to have what he does not have? Where are they written except in the book of that light called Truth, out of which every just law is copied and passes into the heart of man who does justice— passes not by transference but by impression, just as the seal of a ring passes into the wax without leaving the ring? But as for him who does not do justice, seeing nevertheless what is to be done, he is turned away from the light by which he nevertheless is still touched. The man who does not even see how he ought to live sins with more excuse since he does not transgress a law he knows: yet even he at times may feel the touch of truth's omnipresent splendor when he admits the justice of a rebuke.

Chapter 16

Those moved by the reminder to convert again to the Lord from that state of deformity wherein worldly desires conformed them to this world have to receive from the Lord their re-formation, as the Apostle says, "Be not conformed to this world, but be reformed in newness of your mind" (Rom 12:2), the beginning of the image's re-forming must come from him who first formed it. It cannot of itself re-form the self which it could de-form. The Apostle says in another place: "Be renewed in the spirit of your mind, and put on the new man, which has been created according to God in justice and holiness of truth" (Eph 4:23). The words "according to God" agree with what we read elsewhere: "to the image of God" (Gn 1:27). Justice and holiness of truth were lost through sin; hence this image became deformed and discolored. When the same Apostle writes: "In the putting off of the body of flesh" (Col 2:11). Here two different realities are not signified: one flesh and the other body of flesh: but because there are fleshless bodies like the celestial bodies and earthly ones without flesh, Paul uses "body of flesh" for that body which is flesh. And in like manner he uses "spirit of the mind" for the spirit which is mind.

In other texts the image is named more explicitly, as when the same advice is given in other words: "Putting off the old man with his deeds, put on the new man who is renewed in the knowledge of God according to the image of his Creator" (Col 3:9). Therefore, what we read in that other place, "Put on the new man that has been created according to God," means exactly what is said in this place, "Put on the new man, that is being renewed according to the image of him who created him." Where the former text reads, "according to God," the latter reads, "according to the image of his Creator," and where the former reads, "in justice and holiness of truth," in the latter we read, "in the knowledge of God." So the renewal and re-forming of the mind takes place "according to God" or "according to God's image": It is said to be according to God to exclude the supposition that it is according to another creature; and according to God's image, to clarify that the renewal is accomplished there where God's image is, in the mind. Likewise we say of the righteous and the faithful departed that he is dead according to the body but not according to the soul. Dead according to the body means dead with or in the body, and not dead with or in the soul. To call a man beautiful according to the body, or strong according to the body, not according to the mind, is to say that his beauty and strength are not mental but bodily. This manner of speaking is quite common. We are not, therefore, to understand "according to the image of his Creator" as if the image, according to which the mind is renewed, is different from the mind, and as if it is not the mind itself that is renewed.

Chapter 17

Certainly the renewal we are discussing is not accomplished in one moment of conversion like the renewal occurring in the moment of baptism by the forgiveness of all sins, none remaining unforgiven. But it is one thing to recover from a fever, and another to regain one's health after weakness resulting from fever. It is one thing to remove a spear from the body, and another to heal the inflicted wound with treatment that follows. So to begin the cure is to remove the cause of sickness: and this occurs through the forgiveness of sins. There is in addition the healing of the sickness itself, accomplished gradually by progressive renewal of the image. Both are manifest in one text of the Psalm where we read, "Who shows mercy upon all your iniquities," which occurs in baptism; and then, "Who heals all your sicknesses" (Ps 103:3), which refers to daily advances whereby the image is renewed. The Apostle spoke of this in clear words: "If our outer man decays, yet is our inner man renewed from day to day" (2 Cor 4:16)—but he is "renewed" as he said in the previously quoted texts, "in the knowledge of God," that is, "in justice and holiness of truth." He who is thus renewed by daily progressing in the knowledge of God, in justice and holiness of truth, is converting the direction of his love from the temporal to the eternal, from visible to intelligible things, from carnal to spiritual things, trying assiduously to control and reduce all desire for the former and to bind himself by love to the latter. All his success in this depends on divine assistance, for it is God's word that "without me you can do nothing" (Jn 15:5).

When the final day of life reveals a man, in the midst of this progress and growth, holding steadfast to the faith of the Mediator, the holy angels will await him to bring him home to the God whom he has served and by whom he must be perfected; and at the end of the world he will receive an incorruptible body, not for punishment but for glory. For the likeness of God will be perfect in this image only in the perfect vision of God: of which vision the Apostle Paul says: "Now we see through a glass darkly, but then face-to-face" (1 Cor 13:12). And again: "But we with unveiled face beholding the glory of the Lord are transformed into the same image from glory to glory, as from the spirit of the Lord" (2 Cor 3:18). This describes the daily process in those progressing as they should.

Chapter 18

This statement is from the Apostle John: "Beloved, we are now the children of God, and it has not yet appeared what we shall be: but we know that when He appears we shall be like Him, for we shall see Him as He is" (Jn 3:2). This indicates that the full likeness of God is attained in His image only when it has attained the full vision of Him. John's words may indeed be considered as referring to the body's immortality; for also in that we shall be like God, but only like the Son, since He alone in the Trinity took a body in which He died, rose again, and which He bore with Him into heaven. We may also speak here of an image of the Son of God in which we, like Him, shall have an immortal body, conformed in that respect to the image of the Son only, not of the Father nor of the Holy Spirit. For of Him alone do we read and receive with very sound faith that "the Word was made flesh" (Jn 1:14). So the Apostle says: "Whom He foreknew, them He also predestined to be conformed to the image of His Son, that He might be firstborn among many brethren" (Rom 8:29). "Firstborn," in fact, "of the dead," in the words of the same Apostle (Col 1:18)—that death whereby His flesh was sown in dishonor and rose again in glory (1 Cor 15:43). According to this image of the Son, to which we are conformed through immortality in the body, we likewise do that which the same Paul says elsewhere: "As we have borne the image of the earthly, let us also bear the image of Him who is from heaven" (1 Cor 15:49). This means: let us who were mortal according to Adam believe with true faith and sure and steadfast hope that we shall be immortal according to Christ. For thus we can bear the same image now, not yet in vision but through faith, not yet in reality but in hope. Indeed in this context the Apostle was speaking of the resurrection of the body.

Chapter 19

But if we consider that image of which it is written, "Let us make man in our image and likeness" (Gn 1:26), not "in my image" or "in your image," we must believe that man was made in the image of the Trinity; and we have devoted our best efforts to discover and understand this. Therefore in respect to this image we may better interpret John's words: "We shall be like Him, for we shall see Him as He is!" Here the Apostle is speaking of Him of whom he has said: "We are the children of God!"

The immortality of the flesh, moreover, will be made perfect in the moment of resurrection, which, as Paul says, will be "in the twinkling of an eye, at the last trumpet: and the dead shall be raised uncorrupted, and we shall be changed" (1 Cor 15:52). For in the twinkling of an eye there shall rise again before the judgment that spiritual body in strength, incorruption, and glory which now as a natural body is being sown in weakness, corruption, and dishonor. But the image that is being renewed day by day in the spirit of the mind, and in the knowledge of God, not outwardly but inwardly, will be perfected by that vision which shall exist after the judgment as face-to-face—the vision which now is only developing, through a glass darkly (1 Cor 13:12).

We ought to understand the perfecting of the image by these words: "We shall be like Him, for we shall see Him as He is." This is the gift to be given us then when we hear the call: "Come you blessed of my Father, possess the kingdom prepared for you" (Mt 25:34). Then the godless one shall be removed so that he does not see the glory of the Lord, when those on the left hand go into eternal punishment, and those on the right hand go into eternal life. But as the Truth has told us, "This is eternal life, that they may know you the one true God, and Jesus Christ whom you have sent" (Jn 17:3).

This wisdom of contemplation is, I believe, in its strict sense, distinguished in Holy Scripture from knowledge, and called wisdom—a human wisdom, yet coming to man only from God: participating in whom, the reasonable and intellectual mind is able to become wise in truth. At the end of his dialogue *Hortensius*, we see Cicero praising this contemplative wisdom. "If," he says, "we meditate day and night, if we sharpen our understanding which is the mind's eye and take care that it not grow dull, if, that is, we live the life of philosophy, then we may have good hope that although our power of feeling and thinking is mortal and transient, it will be pleasant for us to pass away when life's duties are done. Nor will our death be offensive to us but a repose from living; and if, however, as the greatest and most famous of the ancient philosophers have believed, our souls are eternal and divine, then we may rightly suppose that the more constant a soul has been in following its own course, that is, in the use of reason and zeal in inquiry, and the less it has mingled and involved itself in the vices and delusions of man, so much the easier will be its ascent and return to its heavenly country." Afterward, he adds this final statement to summarize and conclude his discussion: "Therefore, to end this long discourse, after these pursuits have filled our life, if it is our will to pass quietly into nothingness or to go immediately from our present home to another far better one, we should dedicate all our energy and attention to these studies."

I cannot but wonder that so powerful a mind should offer to men who live the life of philosophy the life-giving happiness in the contemplation of truth, a "pleasant passing away" when human life's duties are done, if our power of thinking and feeling is mortal and transient; as though this would be the death and destruction of that which we so little loved or so fiercely hated that its passing away would be pleasant to us. He did not learn that from the philosophers to whom he gives such great praise; his opinion smacked rather of the New Academy, which had led him to skepticism even about the most evident truths. But, as he admits, the tradition that came to him from those philosophers who were the greatest and most famous was that souls are eternal. Indeed, the advice is appropriate for eternal souls so that they may be found at the end of their life "following their own course, that is, in the use of reason and the zeal in inquiry," not "mingling and involving themselves in the vices and delusions of men," so that they may more easily return to God. But for unhappy men, as all men must be whose mortality is supported by reason alone without faith in the Mediator, this course which consists in the love of God and in the search for truth is not enough. I have done my best to demonstrate this in previous books of this treatise, especially the fourth and thirteenth.

The City of God provides a theological view of history. The first five books argue against the pagan opinion that polytheism accounted for the temporal prosperity of the Roman State. The next five books argue against the pagan position that polytheism leads to eternal happiness, a position taken by some Greek Neoplatonic philosophers. The final twelve books place history within the perspective of salvation. Books 11–14 discuss the scriptural facts of human origins, the rise of two cities or societies (heavenly and earthly), and human secular history until A.D. 425. Books 15–18 discuss the progress of the two cities, while books 19–22 describe their ends or eschatology, the four last things: death, judgment, heaven, and hell. Only at the end of the world will it be evident who belongs to the City of God, the society of good men and good angels, and who belongs to the city of the devil, the society of the fallen angels and wicked men.

The greater part of The City of God describes the four pillars of civilization—Roman, Greek, Hebrew, and Christian—and demonstrates the destiny of humankind: heaven or hell according to the objects of one's love: "Two loves have built two cities; self-love in contempt of God has built the earthly city; love of God in contempt of oneself has built the heavenly city."

The struggle between these two cities is the substance of history. The two cities are also commingled in each person, where they are struggling for possession. The consummation of history will be the separation of the two cities into heaven and hell. The doctrine of the resurrection of the body is central to this view. In arguing for it from faith, Augustine clearly manifested his conviction that the body is essential to the human reality. His insistence on personal immortality, made possible by the resurrection of Christ, separated his views from those of Plato, Aristotle, Plotinus, and Porphyry.

Here we present Book 19, on the secular and Christian notions of happiness. Augustine returns to the theme of human desire for God, which he had set forth in the first book of the Confessions and in The Happy Life. He opposes the miseries and passing pleasures of temporal life to the certain happiness of eternal life for those who live by faith. This happiness is peace—peace in eternity or eternity in peace. Peace is the presence of God. His presence in the universe was manifested in the Incarnation, which restored order, the order of love. Happiness, therefore, does not consist in rejecting the world but in learning to love it as it should be loved, for earthly goods can indeed contribute to human peace and to eternal life. Peace with oneself is a true love of self, that is, preferring God to self; this is the model for loving the neighbor. Authorities have much to do with peace. To be themselves happy, authorities are to secure the peace of those whom they serve. In this we recognize that Augustine highly valued the state and saw it able to bring peace to citizens when the rulers themselves were at peace with God. Each city seeks its own peace, yet the citizens of the City of God (an invisible, mystical city) can make use of the intelligent organization of the earthly state as long as the state does not forbid the worship of the One God. No Augustinian theory of the relation between Church and state is given, but Church members have two allegiances—to God and country, with the allegiance to God having priority. As citizens, Christians have responsibilities to their fellow citizens, owing positive charity to pagan neighbors and obligated to promote public concord. A Christian "must not be all for himself, but sociable in his life and actions," so that if asked to assume public office, the law and charity require this.

—MARY T. CLARK

Book Nineteen

Chapter 17

But the families who do not live by faith pursue an earthly peace by means of the good things and conveniences of this temporal life, while a household of those living by faith awaits the everlasting blessings promised for the future, using like pilgrims anything earthly and temporal, not letting them entrap or distract from the path that leads to God, but using them to endure more easily and not to aggravate the burden of the corruptible body which weighs down the soul (Ws 9:15). Therefore, both kinds of human groups and of households use alike whatever is needed for this mortal life, but in using them each has its own quite different end in view. So also the earthly city which lives not by faith seeks an earthly peace, and its aim at the concord of citizens concerning command and obedience is limited to a kind of agreement of human wills in respect to whatever is useful for this mortal life. But the Celestial City, or rather the part of it which goes its pilgrim way in this mortal life and lives by faith, must also use this peace until that mortal state for which such peace is necessary shall pass away. Therefore, as long as it leads its life in captivity, as it were, being a stranger in the earthly city although it has already received the promise of redemption and the gift of the Spirit as pledge of it, it does not hesitate to obey the laws of the earthly city whereby whatever ministers to the support of mortal life is so administered, that since this mortal life is common to both, a harmony may be preserved between both cities concerning the things belonging to it.

Because the earthly city has had certain philosophers whose doctrine is condemned by the Divine Teaching and who, being deceived either by their own conjectures or by demons, supposed that there are many gods to be bribed to support human concerns, and that different provinces belong to different responsibilities of theirs, so that the body is the province of one, the soul of another; and in the body, one rules the head, another the neck, and so forth with each member; likewise in the soul, one presides over natural intelligence, another over education, another over anger, yet another over lust; and so the various affairs of life were assigned; one god cares for cattle, other gods respectively for grain, wine, oil, woods, money, navigation, wars and victories, marriage, birth, fertility, and so forth; but because the Celestial City knew only one God to be worshiped and believed with faithful piety that He is to be served with that service which in Greek is called *latria* and should be rendered only to God, it happens that the Celestial City could not have common laws of religion with the earthly city and on this point must dissent and become a wearisome burden to those who thought differently and must endure their anger and hatred and persecutions, except that the minds of their enemies have been alarmed by the multitude of the Christians and by the divine help accorded them.

While this Celestial City, then, pursues its path as a pilgrim on earth, it calls citizens from all peoples and collects an alien society of all languages, careless as to differences in manners, laws, institutions by which earthly peace is gained or maintained, abolishing or destroying none of it, nay, rather preserving and following them, for however diverse they may be among various nations, they aim at one and the same end, earthly peace, as long as that religion which teaches the obligation to worship one most high and true God is not impeded.

Therefore even the Celestial City in its pilgrimage makes use of the earthly peace and guards and seeks the convergence of human wills concerning what is useful for man's mortal nature as far as sound piety and religion allow, and makes the earthly peace minister to the heavenly peace, which is so truly peace that it must be considered and called the only peace, at least of a rational creature, since it is the best ordered and most harmonious fellowship in the enjoyment of God and one another in God. And when we reach that peace, this mortal life shall give way to one that is eternal; no animal body to weigh down the soul with its corruption, but a spiritual body lacking nothing and subdued in every part to the will. In its pilgrim state the Celestial City possesses this peace by faith; and by this faith it lives justly when it makes the attainment of that peace the aim of every good action in which it engages for the service of God and one's neighbor, since the life of a city is surely a social life.

Chapter 18

As to the uncertainty about everything which Varro alleges to be the differentiating characteristic of the New Academy, the City of God utterly denounces such doubt as madness. About those things which its mind and reason apprehend, it has most certain knowledge, although this knowledge is limited because of the corruptible body that weighs down the spirit (since, as the Apostle says, "we know in part" [1 Cor 13:9]); yet it trusts the evidence of the senses which the mind uses through the agency of the body, since he is miserably deceived who thinks that they should never be trusted. It believes also in the Holy Scriptures, old and new, that we call Canonical, whence comes the very faith by which the just man lives (Heb 2:4); through this faith we walk without doubting as long as we are on pilgrimage exiled from the Lord (2 Cor 5:6). As long as this faith is sound and certain, we may without just reproach doubt about those matters which neither sense nor reason has perceived and which have not been revealed to us by the Canonical Scriptures, and that we have not become aware of through witnesses whom it is absurd not to trust.

Chapter 19

It is unimportant in the City of God whether whoever follows the faith leading to God does so in one dress or manner of life or another as long as these are not against the divine precepts; hence, when philosophers themselves become Christians, they are not forced to change their dress and manner of living, which do not hinder religion, but only their false doctrines. So the peculiarity of the Cynics, which Varro emphasized, is of no concern if nothing indecent or uncontrolled is done. Indeed, of those three kinds of life, the contemplative, the active, and the mixed, although anyone might lead his life in any one of them with faith preserved and attain everlasting rewards, yet there is value in what he possesses through his love of truth, and in what he expends by the claim of Christian love. No one ought to be so entirely contemplative as not to consider his neighbor's benefit or so active as to neglect the contemplation of God. Leisure should not mean delight in dull vacancy of mind but inquiry or discovery of truth so that each one makes progress without withholding from others what he has discovered.

And in action we should not covet the honors and power of this life, since everything under the sun is vanity (Eccl 1:23), but we should aim at using our position and influence if these have been honorably won for the benefit of those who are under us, which is according to God's law, as we have previously explained. For that reason the Apostle says: "He that desires the episcopate desires a good work" (1 Tm 3:1). He wished to show what the word *episcopate* means: a task, not an honor. For it is a Greek word derived from the fact that he who is set over others oversees or cares for them; for *epi* means "over" and *skopein* "to see," and therefore we may, if we choose, translate *episkopein* into Latin as "oversee." So that a bishop who loves to govern rather than to do good is no bishop. And so no one is prohibited from zeal in inquiring into truth because that pertains to a praiseworthy use of leisure; but it is inappropriate to covet high position without which a people cannot be ruled, although the position be held and administered appropriately. Therefore, love of truth seeks holy leisure; the necessity of charity undertakes righteous activity. If no burden is placed on us, we are free to discern

life, whether common to all or our special possession, is such
that it should be called a solace of our misery rather than an
enjoyment of blessedness. Also, our very justice, although it is
true in relation to the true final good to which it is subordinated, is nevertheless in this life only of such a kind as to consist
rather in the remission of sins than in the perfecting of virtues.
Witness the prayer of the entire City of God that is exiled on
earth. Through all its members it cries out to God: "Forgive us
our debts as we forgive our debtors" (Mt 6:12). Nor is this
prayer efficacious for those whose faith is dead without works
(Jas 2:17), but only for those whose faith brings forth works
through love (Gal 5:6). For because the reason, though subjected to God, in this mortal condition and in the corruptible
body, which weighs down the soul (Ws 9:15), does not perfectly rule the vices, such a prayer is necessary for just men. For
although the reason exercises command over the vices, certainly
this is not without struggle. And even if we fight the good fight
and rule as master, after such foes have been defeated and subdued, still in this realm of weakness something creeps in so that
sin is found, if not in some swift action, certainly in some
momentary utterance or some fleeting thought. And therefore
there is no complete peace as long as the vices are being ruled,
because the battle against resisting vices is precarious, while
those conquered do not allow for a triumph of carefree ease but
one held down under a command that is full of anxiety. Among
all these temptations, therefore, of which it has been briefly
asserted in the divine oracles: "Is man's life on earth anything

but temptation?" (Jb 7:1), who will assume that his life is such that he need not say to God: "Forgive us our debts," unless it be a proud man, not truly great, but puffed up and bloated, who is justly resisted by Him who gives grace abundantly to the humble? On this account it is written: "God resists the proud, but gives grace to the humble" (Jas 4:6; 1 Pt 5:5). And so in this life, accordingly, justice for the individual means that God rules and man obeys, the soul rules over the body and reason rules over the vices even when rebellious, whether by subduing or withstanding them, and that from God Himself we seek grace to do our duty and forgiveness for our sins, and that we offer our service of thanksgiving for the blessings received. But in that final peace to which this justice should be subordinated and for the sake of having it this justice should be maintained, since our nature will be healed of its sickness by immortality and incorruption and will have no vices, and since nothing either in ourselves or in another will be at war with any one of us, the reason will not need to rule the vices, since they will no longer exist; but God will rule man; and soul, the body, and in obeying we shall find a pleasure and ease as great as the felicity of our living and reigning. And there, for all and for everyone, this state will be everlasting, and its everlastingness will be certain; and therefore the peace of this blessedness or the blessedness of this peace will be the highest good.

Chapter 28

But, on the other hand, those who do not belong to that City of God will receive everlasting misery, which is called also the

second death (Rv 2:11), because neither the soul that is alien-
ated from God's life can be said to live there nor the body,
which will be subjected to everlasting torments; and this second
death will be all the harder to bear in that it cannot be ended in
death. But since just as misery is the opposite of blessedness,
and death of life, so war is the opposite of peace, the question is
properly raised: what or what kind of war can be understood to
take place in the final state of the wicked to correspond to the
peace that is predicted and lauded in the final state of the righteous? But let the questioner attend to what is harmful or
destructive in warfare, and he will see that it is nothing but the
mutual opposition and conflict of things. Therefore, what war
can he imagine more grievous and bitter than one in which the
will is so opposed to passion and passion to will that their hos-
tilities can be ended by the victory of neither, and in which the
power of pain so struggles with the very nature of the body that
neither yields to the other? For in this life, when such a conflict
arises, either pain conquers, and death takes away feeling, or
nature conquers, and health removes the pain. But in the life
beyond, pain remains to torment and nature stays to feel it; neither ceases to be lest the punishment should also cease.

However, since these are the extremes of good and evil of
which we should seek to gain the former and escape the latter,
and since through judgment good men pass to the former, bad
men to the latter, I will, so far as God may grant, discuss this
judgment in the following book.

THE RULE OF SAINT AUGUSTINE

The evangelical foundation of the Rule is found in the Acts of the Apostles 4:32, where we read that "the whole group of believers were united, heart and soul." And so Augustine tells his brethren: "The main purpose for your having come together is to live harmoniously in your house, intent upon God in oneness of mind and heart" (1.1).

This oneness of mind and heart or interpersonal unity is to be attained through love, a mutual love that enables all to remain "intent upon God." Charity is the environment of monastic life, enabling all to remain under the yoke of the Lord and making the burden ever lighter. In a contemplative atmosphere the monks aim at union with Christ, who lived freely for others. Just as there is a natural union of minds and bodies, so is there a material aspect to the union of minds and hearts in the monastery: this is the holding in common of all material possessions to be distributed according to each one's needs.

Fidelity to regulations that often seem too minute is, however, an effort to purify the heart for the "seeing of God." And regulations concerning common life are directed ultimately toward that inner community of thoughts and affections by which God's love is expressed for each one. As God dwells in the temple of each one's heart, so He dwells within the community as in a temple, to witness to the oneness of Christ and His members. The aim of "living in freedom under grace" remains always the ideal toward which numerous specific rules are directed. Renewal of the religious life in each age requires a reexamination as to whether the inherited regulations are efficacious in achieving the aim of religious life.

To follow the Rule of Saint Augustine is to make a spiritual ascent to that Beauty which is God, the Splendor of Truth. Generosity is the response to this Beauty, which is reflected in a true community of one heart and one mind in the one Christ after the model of the first Christians at Jerusalem. A fervent monastery is a microcosm of the City of God.

Augustine's Rule represents the first monastic legislation, and his first monastery at Thagaste was a lay monastery. Bishop Eusebius of Vercelli (371) had already established community life for the clergy. At Hippo Augustine first established a community of lay monks, and as bishop he formed an episcopal community of priests who renounced personal wealth and marriage while living ascetically and contemplatively and working for the salvation of others in humility, charity, and peace.

—MARY T. CLARK

First and foremost, my very dear Brothers, you are to love God, and then your neighbor, because these are the chief commandments given to us.

I. Mutual Love: Expressed in the Community of Goods and in Humility

1. We urge you who form a religious community to put the following precepts into practice.

2. Above all, live together in harmony (Ps 67:7), having one mind and one heart (Acts 4:32), intent on God, since that is why you have come together.

3. Do not call anything your own but share all things. Food and clothes should be distributed to each one of you by your superior, not to all equally, but to each one according to his need, since all do not enjoy equal health. For this is what you read in the Acts of the Apostles: "All things owned were held in common, and to each one was given whatever he needed" (Acts 4:32, 35).

4. Those who had personal possessions in the world should freely consent when they enter religious life that these become the property of the community.

5. Those, however, who had no personal possessions should not seek in religious life those things which they could not have before they entered. Yet they are to be given whatever is required for their infirmities even though their poverty before they entered religious life prevented their having even life's necessities. Nor should they consider themselves fortunate because they

receive food and clothes which were beyond their means in their previous lives.

6. Nor should those who formerly were poor now become proud because they associate with those whom previously they dared not approach. Instead, let them raise up their hearts and avoid empty earthly vanities lest our communities be useful for the rich and not for the poor: if the rich learn humility there and the poor are puffed up with pride.

7. But, on the other hand, those who were obviously important in the world should not look down upon their brethren who have entered the religious community from a condition of poverty. They should be prouder of their life together with their poor brothers than of the social status of their rich parents. The fact that they have contributed some of their resources to the community is no reason for them to have a high opinion of themselves. Nor should they take greater pride by sharing their riches with the community than by enjoying them in the world. For whereas all vices express themselves in evil acts, pride lurks also in our good works in order to destroy even them. And what good is it to dispense gifts to the poor and even become poor oneself if giving up riches makes a person prouder than he was when he possessed a fortune?

8. Live, then, all of you, "one in mind and one in heart" (Acts 4:32), and mutually honor God in one another because each of you has become His temple (2 Cor 6:16).

II. Community Prayer

1. "Persevere in prayer" (Col 4:2) at the hours and times appointed.

2. In the oratory no one should do anything out of keeping with the purpose of the place. So that if some perhaps have leisure and wish to pray outside the regular hours, they should not be distracted by those wanting to use the oratory for another purpose.

3. When with Psalms and hymns you pray to God, ponder in your heart what your voice utters.

4. When you sing, keep to the text you have, and do not sing what is not intended to be sung.

III. Community and Care of the Body

1. Subdue your body by fasting and by abstaining from food and drink insofar as health permits. Those unable to fast the whole day may take something to eat even apart from the main evening meal. They may do this, however, only around midday. But the sick may take something to eat any time of day.

2. When you come to the table, listen until you leave to the customary reading without disturbance or dispute. Not only are you to satisfy your physical hunger but also to hunger for the word of God (cf. Am 8:11).

3. And if those entering the community who were accustomed to live comfortably have extra nourishment given to them, this should not irritate others or seem unjust to those whose former style of life made them physically stronger. They

should not consider their weaker brothers more favored because they receive a more generous fare; they should rather be glad that they are able to bear what the former cannot yet endure.

4. And if more food, clothing, and bedding are given to those entering the community who were accustomed to live comfortably than is provided for others who are stronger and more fortunate, the latter should be mindful of how much the rich now have to live without in comparison with their previous life even though they cannot live as simply as those who are physically stronger.

5. Nor should all the brethren desire what they see given to a few, for it is given not as a mark of honor but out of consideration for their weakness. Otherwise, there would be undesirable abuse in religious life where the rich become schooled in hardship and the poor become more luxurious. Obviously, the sick should receive special food; if not, their illness would only increase. Even if they entered from the poorest social conditions, they should, when convalescing, receive that treatment most likely to renew their strength. Their illness entitles them to what the rich are entitled to because of their former style of life. But once they have made a complete recovery, they are to resume their previous mode of life when they were happier because their needs were fewer. The simpler a way of life, the better is it suited to the servants of God. Once restored to health, they should not allow the desire for food, previously needed to support their weakness, now to enslave them. Those who can lead simple lives without any difficulty should consider themselves the

most fortunate of people. For it is better to make do with too little than to have many things.

IV. Community Responsibility in Good and Evil

1. There should be nothing that attracts attention in your attire. Try to find favor by your manner of life, not by the clothes you wear.

2. When you go out, go with someone else and stay together when you have reached your destination.

3. In walking, standing, and in all your actions do nothing that might seem offensive, but do that which befits the holiness of your way of life.

4. When you see a woman, do not fix your eyes on her. For although when you go out you are not forbidden to look at women, it is sinful to desire them or to want to be desired by them (cf. Mt 5:28). For it is not only by gestures of affection that desire between men and women is awakened but also by looks. And do not say that you have pure intentions if you keep looking at a woman, because the eye is the messenger of the heart. When impure intentions are allowed to appear not by words but just by exchanging glances and finding pleasure in each other's affection, even though not in each other's arms, we cannot speak any longer of true chastity, which is precisely that of the heart.

5. Let no one who fixes his eye upon a woman and delights in having her eye fixed on him suppose that he is not seen by others; he is certainly seen, and by those he does not realize are observing him. But although his act were hidden and unobserved, how can

he hide anything from that Witness above us from whom nothing is hidden (Prv 24:12)? Or are we to think that He does not see because He sees with a patience as great as His Wisdom? Let the religious man therefore fear to displease God by pleasing a woman wickedly. Let him know that God looks upon all things and so be unwilling to look upon a woman lustfully. For in this respect and for this reason fear was recommended when it was written: "The covetous eye is an abomination to the Lord" (Prv 27:20).

6. When therefore you are together in church or anywhere else where women are present, you are to consider yourselves responsible for one another's chastity. Then God who dwells in you (2 Cor 6:16) will protect you through your responsibility for one another.

7. And if you should notice this wantonness of the eye I have spoken of in a brother, admonish him immediately, so that what was begun will not progress but will be promptly corrected.

8. But if after this warning you see him repeating this on another day, then whoever happens to see this should report him as he would report a wounded brother in need of healing. Yet, first of all, the fault should be pointed out to another, and perhaps to a third so that they may be convinced (Mt 18:15–17). Thus he can be convicted on the testimony of two or three witnesses and punished with suitable severity. Do not consider yourself malicious for reporting this. For surely you are not innocent if by your silence you allow your brothers, whom by reporting you could have healed, to perish. For if your brother had a bodily wound which he wanted to hide because of the fear of surgery,

would it not be cruel for you to remain silent and merciful for you to reveal it? How much more then should you reveal this, lest he suffer a more deadly wound in the heart?

9. But if he fails to heed the admonition, he should first be brought to the attention of the superior before his offense is made public to the others who will have to prove his guilt, if he denies the charge. Thus he may be reproved privately so that his fault may perhaps be kept from others. If, however, he denies the charge, then others should be summoned so that he may be accused in the presence of all, not only by one witness but by two or three (1 Tm 5:20), and thus stand convicted. If proven guilty, he must submit to the punishment imposed by his superior or by the higher authority under whose jurisdiction the matter falls. If he refuses to submit to the punishment and does not voluntarily depart, let him be expelled from your midst. For this is done not out of cruelty but out of mercy, lest he ruin many others by his evil influence.

10. And let what I have said about the restraint of impure looks be diligently and faithfully observed in the discovery, prevention, manifestation, proving, and punishment of all other sins. This should be done out of charity for the neighbor but out of hatred for their sins.

11. But if any of you has so seriously fallen as to have secretly accepted letters or any kinds of gifts from a woman, let him be pardoned and prayed for if he openly confesses his fault. But if he is detected and convicted, he must be more severely punished according to the decision of the superior or higher authority.

V. Service of One Another

1. Your clothes should be kept in one place and looked after by one or more brothers. They will see that they are well aired and kept free of moths. And just as your food is prepared in one kitchen, so your clothes are to come from one storeroom. If possible, have no concern as to what is given you to wear at the change of seasons. It does not matter whether you get back the same clothes you handed in or something worn by another, provided no one is denied what he needs (Acts 4:35). But if among you there arise disputes and murmuring because someone complains about receiving poorer clothing than he previously had and thinks it beneath his dignity not to be as well dressed as this one or that one of his brothers, by this you prove how lacking you are in that holy and inner garment of the heart, you who quarrel over bodily garments. But if your weakness is tolerated so that you receive what you turned in, nevertheless whatever you place aside must be kept in one place under the common charge.

2. This should be done so that no one may seek merely his own convenience but that all may work for the interest of the community with greater zeal and more readiness than if he were providing for his own individual interest. For it has been written of charity that it "is not self-seeking" (1 Cor 13:5), that is to say, it puts the interests of the community before its own interests, and not the other way around. The more you are concerned for the interests of the community rather than for your own interests, the more certain is your progress in the spiritual life. Thus through all the passing needs of men's lives something sublime

and permanent will be revealed, namely, charity (1 Cor 12:31; 13:13).

3. Consequently, a religious who receives clothes or other useful things from his parents or relatives may not keep these quietly for himself. He should give them to the superior so that, as the property of the community, they may be placed at the disposal of whoever needs them (Acts 4:32, 35).

4. When you want to wash your clothes or have them laundered, do so in consultation with the superior, lest an excessive desire for clean clothes defile your souls.

5. Neither shall the body be denied the proper hygienic care according to the requirements of good health. Let the physician's advice be carried out without objections. If anyone refuses to comply, he must, at the superior's command, do what is useful for his health. But if a sick brother desires something that is perhaps not helpful, his wish shall not be fulfilled. At times something is believed helpful because it is pleasant though it may be harmful.

6. Finally, in the case of an ailment which does not externally appear, whatever a servant of God says about his illness should be believed without mistrust. Nevertheless, the physician should be consulted if it is uncertain that the remedy desired is helpful.

7. No fewer than two or three of you together should go to the public baths or elsewhere on necessary business. Nor should he who must go somewhere on business go with the companions he chooses; he ought to go with those whom the superior appoints.

8. The care of the sick and convalescent or those suffering from any weakness of health even without fever should be entrusted to a special brother so that he may procure from the dispensary whatever he deems appropriate in each case.

9. Those charged with the kitchen, clothing, or books should serve their brothers without complaining.

10. Books should be requested at a fixed hour each day. Whoever makes a request outside this time should be refused.

11. But clothes and shoes must be given to those who need them without delay by those in charge.

VI. Unanimity and Forgiveness

1. Let there be no quarrels among you, or, if they arise, end them as quickly as possible, lest your anger grow into hatred and the splinter become a beam (Mt 7:3−5) and make your heart a murderer's den. For we read in the Scriptures: "Whoever hates his brother is a murderer" (1 Jn 3:15).

2. Whoever has offended another by harshly reproaching, insulting, or calumniating him should be quick to make amends, and he who was offended should forgive without reproaches. If, however, the injury has been mutual, both must forgive each other's trespasses (Mt 6:12). And this on account of your prayers, which should be recited with greater sincerity each time you repeat them. He who is quick-tempered yet prompt to ask pardon from one he admittedly offended is better than the one who, although less inclined to anger, finds asking for forgiveness too difficult. He who is never willing to ask pardon or who from his

heart does not do so (Mt 18:35) has no purpose in being in a religious community even though he is not expelled. Take care then to avoid being too harsh in your words; but if they should escape your lips, let those same lips which caused the wound not be ashamed to speak the healing word.

3. Sometimes, however, the need for discipline may require you to speak harshly when correcting young people who have not yet reached adulthood. Even if you think you have been excessive in your language, you are not required to ask forgiveness. For if your conduct toward these young people is too submissive, then your authority, which they should be ready to accept, is undermined. In such cases you should ask forgiveness of the Lord of All who knows how much you love your brothers, even those whom you have perhaps disciplined too severely. Anyway, you are to love one another with a spiritual and not a carnal love.

VII. Love in Authority and Obedience

1. The superior should be obeyed as a father (Heb 13:17), with the respect due him, so that in him you honor God. This is even more true in the case of the priest, who bears responsibility for all of you.

2. It belongs primarily to the superior to see that these rules are all observed and, if some point has been neglected, to see to it that the fault is not carelessly overlooked but corrected and punished. Whatever exceeds the limits of his authority in this matter should be referred to a higher superior.

3. Your superior, however, ought not to seek his happiness in power which enables him to lord it over you (Lk 22:25–26) but in

charity whereby he can be of service to you (Gal 5:13). As a superior, let him be upheld in honor before you; as a servant, let him submit himself in fear before God. Let him be an example to all of good works (Ti 2:7). "Let him restrain the unruly, console the weak, support the sick, be patient with everyone" (1 Thes 5:14). Let him readily uphold discipline while instilling fear. And he should try to be loved by you rather than feared, although both love and respect are necessary. Let him always remember that he will have to account to God for the way he has looked after you (Heb 13:17).

4. By your ready obedience, therefore, you show compassion not only to yourselves (Sir 30:24) but at the same time also to your superior because the higher is his rank among you, so much the greater is his danger.

VIII. Observance of the Rule

1. May the Lord grant that you joyfully observe all these rules as lovers of spiritual beauty. Send forth the good odor of Christ (2 Cor 2:15) by your good way of living, not as those enslaved under the law but as those liberated under grace (Rom 6:14–22).

2. This little book is to be read to you once a week. As in a mirror, you will be able to see in it whether there is anything you are neglecting or forgetting (Jas 1:23–25). And when you find that you are doing what has been written here, give thanks to the Lord, the Giver of all good. But if anyone finds that he has failed on any point, let him repent for the past and be vigilant for the future. Let him pray: Forgive me my trespasses and lead me not into temptation (Mt 6:12–13).

ABOUT THE EDITOR

HarperCollins Spiritual Classics Series Editor Emilie Griffin has long been interested in the classics of the devotional life. She has written a number of books on spiritual formation and transformation, including *Clinging: The Experience of Prayer* and *Wilderness Time: A Guide to Spiritual Retreat*. With Richard J. Foster she coedited *Spiritual Classics: Selected Readings on the Twelve Spiritual Disciplines*. Her latest book is *Wonderful and Dark Is this Road: Discovering the Mystic Path*. She is a board member of Renovaré and leads retreats and workshops throughout the United States. She and her husband William live in Alexandria, Louisiana.

ABOUT FRANCINE DU PLESSIX GRAY

Francine du Plessix Gray is a regular contributor to *The New Yorker*, and the author of numerous books of fiction and nonfiction including *Simone Weil*, *At Home with the Marquis de Sade: A Life*, *Rage and Fire*, *Lovers and Tyrants*, *Soviet Women*, and most recently *Them: A Memoir of Parents*. She lives in Connecticut.

THE CLASSICS OF **WESTERN SPIRITUALITY**
A LIBRARY OF THE GREAT SPIRITUAL MASTERS

These volumes contain original writings of universally acknowledged teachers within the Catholic, Protestant, Eastern Orthodox, Jewish, Islamic, and American Indian traditions.

The Classics of Western Spirituality unquestionably provide the most in-depth, comprehensive, and accessible panorama of Western mysticism ever attempted. From the outset, the Classics has insisted on the highest standards for these volumes, including new translations from the original languages, and helpful introductions and other aids by internationally recognized scholars and religious thinkers, designed to help the modern reader to come to a better appreciation of these works that have nourished the three monotheistic faiths for centuries.

Athanasius	*Francis and Clare*	*Pietists*	*Augustine of Hippo*
Edited and Introduced	Edited and Introduced	Edited and Introduced	Edited and Introduced
by Robert C. Gregg	by Regis J. Armstrong and	by Peter C. Erb	by Mary T. Clark
0-8091-2295-2 $19.95	Ignatius C. Brady	0-8091-2509-9 $22.95	0-8091-2573-0 $24.95
	0-8091-2446-7 $17.95		

For more information on the
CLASSICS OF WESTERN SPIRITUALITY, contact Paulist Press
(800) 218-1903 • **www.paulistpress.com**